access to history

The CIVIL WARS 1640–9

Second Edition

D0264299

Angela Anderson

Hodder & Stoughton

A MEMBER OF THE HODDER HEADLINE GROUP

Acknowledgements

The Publishers would like to thank the following for permissions to reproduce material in this volume:

Hodder Arnold for extracts from *Authority and Conflict* by Derek Hirst and *The Outbreak of the English Civil War* by Anthony Fletcher; Thomson Publishing Services for extracts from *The Causes of the English Revolution*, by Lawrence Stone and *The Debate on the English Revolution Revisited*, by R.C. Richardson both published by Routledge.

The publishers would like to thank the following for permission to reproduce copyright illustrations in this volume:

Hulton-Deutsch Collection/CORBIS: p.6; Michael Nicholson/CORBIS: p.26; The Fotomas Index: p.40 (top and bottom), p.92 (top and bottom), p.109; National Portrait Gallery: p.68; British Library: p. 120; Scottish National Portrait Gallery/collection of Earl of Rosebury, Dalment House: p.151

Every effort has been made to trace and acknowledge ownership of copyright. The Publishers will be glad to make suitable arrangements with any copyright holders whom it has not been possible to contact.

Orders: please contact Bookpoint Ltd, 130 Milton Park, Abingdon, Oxon OX14 4SB. Telephone (44) 01235 827720, Fax: (44) 01235 400454. Lines are open from 9.00–6.00, Monday to Saturday, with a 24-hour message answering service. Email address: orders@bookpoint.co.uk

British Library Cataloguing in Publication Data
A catalogue record for this title is available from the British Library

ISBN 0 340 85037X

First published 2002
Impression number   10 9 8 7 6 5 4 3 2 1
Year   2007 2006 2005 2004 2003

Copyright © 2002 Angela Anderson

Cover illustration shows Henry Ireton attributed to Robert Walker, (courtesy of the National Portrait Gallery).
Typeset by Fakenham Photosetting Limited, Fakenham, Norfolk
Printed in Great Britain for Hodder & Stoughton Educational, a division of Hodder Headline, 338 Euston Road, London NW1 3BH by Bath Press Ltd.

Contents

Preface

To the general reader

Although the *Access to History* series has been designed with the needs of students studying the subject at higher examination levels very much in mind, it also has a great deal to offer the general reader. The main body of the text (i.e. ignoring the 'Study Guides' at the ends of chapters) forms a readable and yet stimulating survey of a coherent topic as studied by historians. However, each author's aim has not merely been to provide a clear explanation of what happened in the past (to interest and inform): it has also been assumed that most readers wish to be stimulated into thinking further about the topic and to form opinions of their own about the significance of the events that are described and discussed (to be challenged). Thus, although no prior knowledge of the topic is expected on the reader's part, she or he is treated as an intelligent and thinking person throughout. The author tends to share ideas and possibilities with the reader, rather than passing on numbers of so-called 'historical truths'.

To the student reader

Although advantage has been taken of the publication of a second edition to ensure the results of recent research are reflected in the text, the main alteration from the first edition is the inclusion of new features, and the modification of existing ones, aimed at assisting you in your study of the topic at AS level, A level, Higher and International Baccalaureate. Two features are designed to assist you during your first reading of a chapter. The *Points to Consider* section following each chapter title is intended to focus your attention on the main theme(s) of the chapter, and the issues box following most section headings alerts you to the question or questions to be dealt with in the section. The *Working on ...* section at the end of each chapter suggests ways of gaining maximum benefit from the chapter.

There are many ways in which the series can be used by students studying History at a higher level. It will, therefore, be worthwhile thinking about your own study strategy before you start your work on this book. Obviously, your strategy will vary depending on the aim you have in mind, and the time for study that is available to you.

If, for example, you want to acquire a general overview of the topic in the shortest possible time, the following approach will probably be the most effective:

1. Read chapter 1. As you do so, keep in mind the issues raised in the *Points to Consider* section.
2. Read the *Points to Consider* section at the beginning of chapter 2 and decide whether it is necessary for you to read this chapter.
3. If it is, read the chapter, stopping at each heading or sub-heading to note

down the main points that have been made. Often, the best way of doing this is to answer the question(s) posed in the Key Issues boxes.
4. Repeat stage 2 (and stage 3 where appropriate) for all the other chapters.

If, however, your aim is to gain a thorough grasp of the topic, taking however much time is necessary to do so, you may benefit from carrying out the same procedure with each chapter, as follows:

1. Try to read the chapter in one sitting. As you do this, bear in mind any advice given in the *Points to Consider* section.
2. Study the flow diagram at the end of the chapter, ensuring that you understand the general 'shape' of what you have just read.
3. Read the *Working on...* section and decide what further work you need to do on the chapter. In particularly important sections of the book, this is likely to involve reading the chapter a second time and stopping at each heading and sub-heading to think about (and probably to write a summary of) what you have just read.
4. Attempt the *Source-based questions* section. It will sometimes be sufficient to think through your answers, but additional understanding will often be gained by forcing yourself to write them down.

When you have finished the main chapters of the book, study the 'Further Reading' section and decide what additional reading (if any) you will do on the topic.

This book has been designed to help make your studies both enjoyable and successful. If you can think of ways in which this could have been done more effectively, please contact us. In the meantime, we hope that you will gain greatly from your study of History.

Keith Randell & Robert Pearce

1 The Origins of the Wars

POINTS TO CONSIDER

The purpose of this chapter is to explain the causes of the crisis that enveloped Charles in 1640, but that is not the same as explaining the causes of war. The crisis created circumstances in which the war became possible, but not necessarily likely and certainly not inevitable. Given that Charles inherited a peaceful kingdom in 1625, it would be easy to assume that he played a major part in its causes, but it is possible that the appearance of tranquility was deceptive, and that tensions and difficulties were already mounting beneath the surface. In reading this chapter you should try to establish a clear picture of the problems that Charles I inherited, and of how his handling of them created a crisis in government in 1640.

1 The Origins of the Crisis

a) The Legacy of the English Reformation

> **KEY ISSUE** In what ways did the Reformation of the 1530s contribute to the development of a crisis between King and Parliament?

Many historians argue that the roots of the seventeenth century crisis lie in the Protestant Reformation that took place in England a century earlier, when King Henry VIII seized control of the Church in England and declared himself to be its head in place of the Pope in Rome. He was able to do this because a German monk named Martin Luther had successfully challenged the Pope's authority in Germany, and Luther's supporters (known as **Protestants**) had carried his ideas to England and other countries. Henry was no Protestant – his interest lay in the power and wealth that he could gain from the Church – but he called on Protestant support and enabled Protestants to gain powerful positions in the new Church of England. This was to have considerable significance for the future. By denying the authority of the Pope, Protestants had to rely on the Bible to provide rules and guidance in religion, and the Bible could be interpreted in different ways. By assuming control of the Church, Henry took on the power, and therefore the responsibility for deciding between competing interpretations, and for enforcing his decisions in matters of conscience.

The Reformation in England is symbolised by three significant events: the Act of Supremacy (1534), the publication of the Bible in

English (1537) and the dissolution of the monasteries in 1536–9. The Act of Supremacy gave Henry VIII supreme power over the doctrine and organisation of the Church. Kings had always been able to influence appointments and call on the help of the Church in government, but Henry now claimed the kind of spiritual authority that allowed him to decide what beliefs were acceptable, and how they should be reflected in the daily services and ceremonies that were to be used. The Act made his power legally enforceable by Act of Parliament, the highest form of law in England. This meant that the King could punish anyone who refused to accept his authority in religion, but it also meant that future monarchs could only change the situation by passing a new Act of Parliament. Therefore, when Henry's son Edward introduced a new Protestant order of service in 1549, and when his daughter Mary tried to restore the authority of the Pope in 1554, they both needed the support of parliaments to make the changes enforceable. By the time Henry's second daughter, Elizabeth, became queen in 1558, there had been a long series of parliamentary settlements involving the Church, royal power, and even the succession to the throne.

The dissolution of the monasteries in 1536–9 transferred most of the wealth of the Church into the hands of the laity (non-clergy). The monasteries had been immensely rich, owning about one-third of all the land in England, and with this land went control of many parish livings and their tithes (a tax of about 10 per cent paid by the people of the parish to provide an income for the local priest or minister). All of this wealth was transferred to the King, but in order to secure the support of the nobility and gentry for the changes that he was making, Henry granted a proportion of it to his servants and supporters. He also sold a great deal of land to pay for his wars against Scotland and France, with the result that much of the monastery land passed into the hands of the nobility, gentry, and even wealthy merchants and farmers who were benefiting from the growth of trade and rising prices. By the end of the sixteenth century the landed gentry of England were more wealthy and numerous than ever before.

They were also better-educated and more important in government than at any previous time. Following the Reformation, the intensely personal and Bible-based Protestant faith spread in England. If knowledge of God came from the Bible rather than the Pope, people wanted to be able to read it for themselves. The spread of grammar schools brought an end to the Church monopoly of education, and widened access to schooling for the laity as a whole. The loss of monks and religious orders meant that royal administration became increasingly reliant on laymen, increasing job opportunities and access to wealth, especially for those with some legal knowledge. To enforce royal authority across the country, the Tudors relied greatly on local magistrates named Justices of the Peace. They were both legal and administrative officials, dealing with such things as licensing ale-houses and upkeep of roads, as well as combatting minor crime. More and more of the gentry were appointed to carry out such duties in each county. Although the post was unpaid, it carried considerable prestige and an enhanced status in the local community. It was therefore highly prized, and many of the gentry were encouraged to study law and the classics in order to equip themselves for such a role.

While none of these developments were entirely new (literacy rates had been rising for some time) there is little doubt that the effects of the Reformation increased and intensified them. The combination of opportunity and incentive encouraged the development of a more numerous, more literate and more articulate class of gentry who shared the responsibility for government with the monarch and the greater nobility, at both local and central levels. Educated at home or in a grammar school, it became customary for them to spend a short period at one of the two universities (Oxford and Cambridge) and later at the Inns of Court [law schools] in London, in order to prepare for their role as managers of land, tenants, law and administration in the local community. The more ambitious and the more needy might well extend their studies and pursue a career in law or administration, but even those who chose not to do so had some knowledge of these areas, and the confidence that came with it. When such men were called, as they periodically were, to attend a parliament and assist the monarch in matters of state, they were certainly capable of expressing their views and offering advice, welcome or not.

In political terms, therefore, the effect of the Reformation in England was to increase the power of both monarch and parliaments. The King had taken control of the Church, becoming the head of government in both Church and State. He claimed to be God's deputy on earth, with sole power over his people. With its office in every parish, the Church represented a vast propaganda machine, its pronouncements backed by the authority of God himself, and it was now entirely at the monarch's disposal. At the same time, however, the changes had been enacted through parliaments. Parliaments represented the nobility and gentry, with a limited input from the merchants and yeomen [independent farmers]. The events of the Reformation and the changes that followed had made parliaments a more necessary part of government, and involved the ruling class across the country in the enactment of momentous changes at the heart of government. A 'political nation' had been forged in the partnership between the monarch and the ruling class, to the benefit of both and at the expense of the Church. However, if the partners were to seriously disagree, for example over the matters of conscience in religion for which the monarch now took responsibility, it would become apparent that parliament's capacity for obstruction had increased in proportion to its role and powers.

b) The Reign of Elizabeth, 1558–1603

When Elizabeth I became queen in 1558, she inherited a weakened and divided kingdom. Her father's last years were dominated by war in Scotland and factional divisions at Court. At his death the Protestant faction [a group of nobles and courtiers who had personal and political links] assumed control and carried through a religious revolution in the Church, but the death of Edward in 1553 allowed Mary to reverse the settlement and restore the authority of the Pope. As the daughter of Catherine of Aragon, whose divorce had occasioned the break with Rome, she had remained a devout Catholic. Supported by her Spanish husband, Philip, she set out to re-convert England, by force if necessary. The public burnings of nearly 300 men, women and children demonstrated that Protestant ideas had taken root in some places, and could only be eradicated by the use of force. A further 800 Protestants fled abroad to Protestant Europe, where their faith hardened and strengthened while they awaited the opportunity to return. Meanwhile, Mary entered a disastrous war against France in support of Spanish interests, which ended in defeat and the loss of England's last continental possession, the port of Calais.

Elizabeth's first priority, therefore, was to bring about a settlement of religious quarrels which could be widely accepted, and to strengthen her own grip on power. As the daughter of Anne Boleyn, her own legitimacy required a Protestant settlement, since the Catholic Church had never recognized her father's divorce and her mother's marriage. At the same time, she was aware that many of her subjects liked and enjoyed the traditional ceremonies used in the Catholic Church. She therefore sought to establish a compromise. In 1559 the Act of Uniformity was passed by parliament, despite the opposition of Mary's bishops in the House of Lords, and established a new Church of England with the queen as Supreme Governor (as a woman she could not claim to be Head of a Church that did not allow women to become priests). The Church was to be run by Bishops, who would advise the queen and enforce her decisions over doctrine and organisation. In doctrinal terms her preferences were clearly Protestant, but she maintained many of the familiar symbols and ceremonies such as the wearing of clerical robes. Above all, the queen demanded obedience to the forms and set prayers contained in a revised Prayer Book, which instructed the clergy on the appropriate services for use on all occasions.

After 30 years of religious changes, mainly enacted through parliament, the Elizabethan Settlement of 1559 sought to create peace by establishing a middle way between Catholic and Protestant ideas, combining Protestant doctrines with more traditional ceremonies and organisation. It was acceptable to the majority, but came under attack from minorities at both ends of the religious spectrum. A

Catholic minority continued to worship in the traditional way, often in private houses. Many were loyal to Elizabeth, but in 1570 their position was made more difficult when the Pope declared Elizabeth a heretic and ordered them to work for her death and replacement by her Catholic cousin, Mary, Queen of Scots. Thereafter, Catholic plots against the queen and the threat of Spanish invasion combined to create strong anti-Catholic feeling. This was fuelled by memories of the burning of Protestants by Queen Mary, and John Foxe's *Acts and Monuments*, which recounted the story of their martyrdom, became essential reading for English Protestants after its publication in 1563. This also increased support for the extreme Protestant minority whose demands for further purification of the Church gave them the nickname of 'puritan'.

The main purpose of the Puritans was to rid the English Church of any trace of the corrupting influence of Popery, which they regarded as an evil force dedicated to the destruction of true religion. They identified the Pope as the anti-Christ, a servant of the devil, who had corrupted and distorted early Christianity into the superstition of medieval Catholicism, hidden the truth of the Bible in an unreadable language [Latin] and prevented thousands of souls from finding God. Only by removing all unnecessary rituals and replacing them with preaching and spontaneous prayer could true religion be protected from such contagion. In Elizabeth's eyes, however, this would mean the delegation of control in the Church from herself to the individual minister – a notion that she regarded with horror. When the Archbishop of Canterbury, Edmund Grindal, demonstrated sympathy with some of these ideas, Elizabeth suspended him from office.

Frustrated by the queen's opposition to further change, these Puritans turned to their sympathisers in parliament, who introduced legislation to reform the Church in various ways. These schemes were based on the ideas published by Thomas Cartwright (a Cambridge scholar) in 1570, which envisaged a Presbyterian system for the Church [see Definitions on p. 7]. To the anger of Puritan MPs who claimed that parliament had a right to debate such matters, these bills were vetoed by the queen. While she accepted that MPs had a right to free speech in their debates, this did not extend to choosing what subjects to raise, or to introducing laws that affected matters of state – such matters were for her alone. Thus the issue of religious reform raised arguments and debates about the relative powers and privileges of monarch and parliament. Meanwhile the queen set out to destroy Puritan influence in the Church. When Grindal died in 1583 she appointed an uncompromising disciplinarian, John Whitgift as Archbishop of Canterbury, and supported his campaign of persecution against puritans who would not conform to the rules of the Prayer Book. In 1590, Cartwright and others were brought before the Church courts and forced to obey. Thus puritanism was contained, but it was not destroyed, and hopes of further reform continued to motivate a minority who were particularly vocal in parliament.

POETRY, POPERY AND THE PROTESTANT QUEEN – THE ELIZABETHAN MYTHOLOGY

-*Profile*-

One of Elizabeth's political skills was her ability to exploit her greatest disadvantage and make it a political asset – her feminity. As a queen in a man's world she needed male support. She obtained it by exploiting her youth and beauty at the time of her accession, to build an image of the Virgin Queen, alone and vulnerable in a hostile environment. In fact, she was a determined and skilful politician, but the image was conveyed to her subjects through the romantic poetry of her courtiers, her portraits and her regular progresses around her kingdom. In the context of a genuine Catholic threat, revealed by a succession of plots against her and the attempt by the Spanish to invade in 1588, she came to symbolize the nation itself, alone in a hostile Catholic Europe. As with any good propaganda, there was enough truth to make the mythology acceptable. The result was a growing sense of national identity based on intense loyalty to the queen, the equation of freedom with the Protestant faith, and a fear of Roman Catholicism [Popery] that bordered on paranoia. While many English Catholics were recognized to be loyal, others were seen as spies and traitors, part of an international conspiracy against England and true religion, centred on Rome and bankrolled by Spanish wealth and power. These perceptions formed a central part of the Tudor legacy to the Stuart kings, and did much to shape political developments in the years before the Civil Wars.

1568:	Rebellion of the Northern Earls, attempting to place Mary Queen of Scots on the throne.
1570:	Elizabeth excommunicated by the Pope and declared deposed from the throne.
1571:	Ridolfi Plot on behalf of Mary, backed by Spain.
1583–4:	Throckmorton Plot on behalf of Mary, backed by Spain.
1586–7:	Babbington Plot and execution of Mary, Queen of Scots.
1588:	The Spanish Armada; beginning of a war with Spain that lasted until 1604.

Definition Box

There are a number of religious terms and labels that historians use in explaining the quarrels over the Church in this period. The term **Anglican** relates to the Church of England, and is used to refer to the broad mainstream of opinion that accepted, and increasingly valued, the compromise established in the Elizabethan settlement. For many ministers and laymen [non-clergy] the combination of Protestant doctrines and traditional ceremonies represented an orderly form of worship based on acceptable rituals, without unnecessary superstition. The range of opinion covered by the term merged into Puritan ideas on the one hand, and extended on the other extreme to a small High Church party, often labelled **Arminian,** who wanted to see greater emphasis on clerical authority and communal rituals similar to those used in the Catholic Church.

The term **Puritan** is best defined as an extreme Protestant view, held by men who feared and disliked any trace of Catholic tradition in the Church, and therefore wanted to simplify the appearance of churches and the services held in them. They emphasised the importance of preaching, private prayer and Bible reading, in establishing a direct relationship with God and a strong personal faith. These views were not different from the mainstream ideas put forward by sixteenth-century Protestants, and adopted by the Church of England, but they were held in a more intense form by those labelled Puritan, and associated with a strong hatred of the Roman Catholic Church, which they regarded as an evil, corrupting influence. Hence they wanted to reform the Church to protect it from Catholic infiltration. They also believed that God ordered the world according to a plan, in which he had **pre-destined** some souls to be saved while others would go to Hell. Those who were to be saved, the 'elect' or 'godly' people, were recognised by their willingness to dedicate themselves to serving God, according to his Will, or **Providence**, which could be discovered by studying the Bible. To feel that you were a part of this group gave great hope and comfort, and led to a dedicated, focused approach to religion. It also meant that access to a teaching Church with a strong ministry was essential.

A **Presbyterian** Church was the preferred version of many puritans, who believed that it offered the best alternative to Popery. Bishops would be abolished, or their powers greatly reduced. Control of the Church would be in the hands of parish ministers who would maintain discipline with the help of lay supporters (Elders). Their duties would include preaching, teaching about the Bible, and overseeing the morality of their parishioners. While government control of the Church would be reduced, clerical control of the local congregations would produce a disciplined and orderly society. This system had been developed by John Calvin in Geneva and established in Scotland by John Knox in 1568. Many English puritans wanted to see a similar system in England, but not all of them went this far. The English merchants and gentry were used to having some influence over their local churches, and often helped to choose the minister because they had bought monastery land or inherited the right to collect tithes. They wanted to keep these powers. On the other hand, there were a few enthusiasts who, already moving in a much more radical direction, argued that a personal faith could only be practised voluntarily, in separate [**separatist**] congregations. The one thing that the queen, bishops, ministers and ruling class agreed upon, was the danger represented by such uncontrolled activists.

By 1603, therefore, the last 70 years of Tudor rule had brought significant change to English government and society. The Monarchy had been strengthened and the Church brought under its control. The old military nobility and knights had developed into educated governors and administrators, working in partnership with the monarch as a political and social elite, to maintain peace, law and order in the localities. Supported by a national Church, and able to assemble as a national ruling class in the occasional meetings of parliament, they had developed a sense of national identity based on English laws, traditions and the Protestant religion. For forty years the queen had symbolised that identity and drawn on the loyalty of her subjects to strengthen the institutions of Tudor monarchy, but beneath the surface there were tensions and uncertainties as to how those institutions should evolve, and how the ruling partnership should develop in a new era. The last decade of Elizabeth's reign was darkened by war, financial problems and bad harvests. The peaceful accession of James VI of Scotland, a Protestant with healthy sons who became James I of England in 1603, offered a promising new start.

2 The Development of the Crisis

a) James I and VI: Finance, Religion and War

KEY ISSUES What problems did James I experience in his relationship with parliament? How far did James create these difficulties?

James I succeeded to the throne in 1603, inheriting religious tensions and rather more severe financial problems, which were increased by his tendency towards extravagance. Although there were complaints about his lavish gifts to friends, especially those who accompanied him from Scotland, this merely added to a much deeper problem. Throughout the sixteenth century a rapidly rising population caused inflation across the whole of Europe, and the underlying problem of rising prices was made much worse by the costs of war. Despite Elizabeth's efforts to avoid it, the war with Spain added greatly to the financial difficulties of the Crown, so that James inherited a debt of over £100,000. More seriously, Elizabeth had sought to avoid difficulties with parliament by selling crown lands rather than ask for parliamentary taxation, and had also failed to update assessments in line with rising prices. The result was that when James did ask for subsidies from parliament, they rarely raised as much as was expected or even necessary.

Financial problems were therefore a major cause of tension between King and parliaments in the reign of James. He continued Elizabeth's unpopular practice of selling monopoly licences, giving one group an exclusive right to trade in certain commodities, until parliament passed an Act against monopolies in 1624. His attempts to add to his revenue by increasing customs duties led to clashes with MPs over both money and privilege – while merchants complained about the new duties, other MPs questioned whether the King had the right to impose them without consulting a parliament. In 1606 the judges decided in the King's favour, and in 1608 a new Book of Rates was published, leading to protests when parliament met in 1610. These unresolved difficulties encouraged parliament to refuse to grant the customary lifetime right to collect Tunnage and Poundage (customs duties) to Charles I upon his accession in 1625. At the same time James's indulgent attitudes to personal favourites and a number of scandals involving the king's friends created a perception that the Court was not only extravagant but also corrupt. In these circumstances parliaments were often reluctant to grant taxes, and increasingly likely to demand a measure of accountability from the king's advisers, if not from the monarch himself.

In the early years of the reign, James also clashed with parliaments over his ambition to unite England and Scotland in a 'perfect union', that would involve adopting the best practices from both kingdoms. English MPs refused to consider the possibility that Scottish methods could offer any benefits. They were also concerned that James's interpretation of the Divine Right by which kings ruled could pose a threat to English laws and liberties. In a book published in 1598, *The True Law of Free Monarchies*, he advanced extravagant claims that 'Kings are as Gods upon the earth'. A careful reading of his philosophical arguments reveals that he fully recognized the limits of royal power, and in practice James was usually careful to respect parliamentary rights, but the initial impression was undeniably damaging.

Nevertheless, James often displayed good judgement and political skill in handling his new subjects. By 1607 he had abandoned his efforts to create greater uniformity across his kingdoms, contenting himself with gradually persuading the Scots to accept the appointment of Bishops in their Church to bring their practice closer to that of the English. A similar measure of tact avoided worsening religious tensions. Although he quarrelled with the Puritan ministers who were still seeking reform in the Church, and made it clear that he intended to continue Elizabeth's reliance on Bishops to exert royal control, James gradually developed a practical compromise that allowed different factions to co-exist within a broad Anglican framework. From time to time the remaining Catholics were subject to heavy fines for not attending Church, from time to time the Puritan ministers who failed to wear the correct robes or use the rituals and ceremonies prescribed by the Prayer Book were brought before the Church courts and punished, but for long periods they were permitted to function undisturbed. The result was that while they continued to work for change, they did so from within the framework of the existing settlement. By this pragmatic approach James was able to achieve a significant measure of harmony.

Unfortunately for the monarchy, his efforts were partly undone in the years after 1618 by events beyond the shores of England and beyond his control. In 1618–21 religious civil war broke out in Germany, and James's son-in-law was centrally involved. The anti-Catholic paranoia that was never far from the surface in seventeenth-century England erupted in a fury, to undermine the precarious religious harmony that James had nurtured. Both family ties and religious loyalties demanded positive action from England, the largest Protestant state in Europe. Unable to afford effective military intervention, James tried a complicated diplomatic plan, involving a partnership with Catholic Spain to bring about peace through mediation. In the process, however, he quarrelled bitterly with parliament in 1621, when, in the course of granting the king money to pursue his plans, MPs invaded his royal prerogatives by debating foreign policy. He was further humiliated in 1622–3 when his son Charles and his favourite, the Duke of Buckingham, embarked on a disastrous, un-invited visit to the Spanish Court in Madrid. By 1624 when they returned, James was faced with a violently Protestant parliament and a furious son and heir, both demanding action against Spain. The old, and increasingly sick King was unable to resist, and in the winter of 1624–5 he agreed to send both an army to intervene in Germany, and a naval expedition to the Spanish port of Cadiz. In the hands of Charles and Buckingham, both proved to be expensive failures, but the effects were not felt by James. In March 1625 he died, leaving Charles to inherit a war that was largely of his own making.

THE ROLE AND DEVELOPMENT OF PARLIAMENTS   *-Profile-*

> All experience shows that the prerogatives of princes may easily and do grow daily, [but] the privileges of the subject are, for the most part, at an everlasting stand. They may be by good providence and care preserved, but once being lost are not recovered but with much disquiet. From the *Commons Apology*, of 1604.

While there is broad agreement among historians that the effects of the Reformation increased the power and status of parliaments, there are many differences over the pace and extent of the changes. Sir John Neale, who studied the parliaments of Elizabeth, argued that her reign saw the emergence of an organised faction in the House of Commons, which he termed the 'Puritan choir', which was consciously seeking greater powers to influence government in both Church and state. Nineteenth-century historians like S.R. Gardiner attributed a major role in causing the Civil War to the attempts of a forward-looking Commons to extend the role of parliaments and limit the powers of a monarchy, which was tending towards absolutism. In support of these claims they pointed to quarrels with Elizabeth over religion and free speech, and to protests directed at James after 1603 [see date list]. There were certainly some successes for parliaments, which were able to use the monarch's need for parliamentary taxation to obtain redress of their grievances [see date list]. All of these measures restricted royal power. It is also clear from the growing number of contested elections in the later sixteenth century, and the increasing tendency for members of the landed gentry to sit as MPs for local boroughs [towns that had a right to send MPs to parliament] that parliamentary seats were becoming more highly regarded and sought after. This would suggest that parliaments were seen as important, and that the gentry were competing to take part.

However, recent research, such as the work of M.A.R. Graves: *Elizabethan Parliaments, 1559–1601* has challenged the extent to which MPs were either organised or forward-looking. In Elizabeth's reign their attempts to reform the Church, influence the succession and extend their rights of free speech all failed. The Commons *Apology* of 1604 suggests a defensive mentality rather than an attempt to extend parliamentary power. Until 1621 James conceded very little, and the concessions made thereafter owed a great deal to the influence of Charles and Buckingham, in their search for support for a war with Spain. What is perhaps most apparent is that quarrels over royal powers and parliamentary privilege rarely began as such – they usually arose from other, more immediate issues, in which strong views and deep-seated fears led MPs to encroach on royal prerogatives as in 1621, or the monarch to over-react to parliamentary debates. The role of parliament in the political and religious changes of the sixteenth century encouraged the view that MPs should be influential in matters of state, while the social, economic and financial changes that were apparent by 1603 increased their opportunities to do so.

Consider the events listed here [and explained in the text] to decide whether the power of parliament was increasing in this period, and how far these developments should be considered part of a deliberate or conscious attempt to change the balance of power in government.

1566: MPs discussed the question of who should succeed Elizabeth.

1576: the MP Peter Wentworth demanded greater freedom of speech in parliament. He was imprisoned in the Tower of London on Elizabeth's orders.

1586: MPs secured the right of the Commons to decide a disputed election result in Norfolk; this had always been done by the Lord Chancellor.

1593: MPs discussed a bill to reform the Church. Elizabeth forbade them to debate it, sparking further arguments over free speech.

1601: MPs successfully withheld taxation until Elizabeth promised to end the selling of monopolies.

1604: James and parliament quarrelled over who should decide a disputed election in Buckinghamshire. The Commons asserted their rights in an *Apology*. James allowed the issue to drop.

1614: MPs protests at attempts by the Court to influence elections to parliament led to the abandonment of the session without granting taxes to the king.

1621: courtiers and advisers, including the Lord Chancellor, were impeached [tried] in parliament for corruption.

1621: a bitter quarrel over whether MPs could debate foreign policy led the Commons to assert their right to complete freedom of debate in a *Protestation*. James refused to accept it, and dissolved parliament.

1624: Charles and Buckingham persuaded the king to assent to an Act against the selling of monopolies, in order to obtain taxes for war with Spain. They also allowed MPs to debate the conduct of the war, to appoint commissioners to supervise the use of money from taxation, and agreed to concentrate on a naval war rather than a land war in Germany.

b) Charles I and the Development of Conflict

> **KEY ISSUES** In what ways did the personality and beliefs of
> Charles I contribute to the developing conflict. Why did the
> problems that he inherited in 1625 develop into a crisis by 1640?

i) King and parliaments, 1625–9

The situation that Charles inherited in 1625 was not an easy one. He
was already at war, and although he had promised to concentrate on
a naval campaign, his honour and his concern for his sister required
intervention in Germany. The army sent under the leadership of a
German mercenary, Count Mansfeld, was inadequately equipped,
and proved an expensive failure. The attempt to negotiate a Spanish
marriage, for which he had made his disastrous visit to Madrid, had
failed in humiliating fashion. Instead, Buckingham, who was now
firmly established as Charles's favourite, negotiated a marriage for
Charles with Henrietta Maria, the Catholic sister of the King of
France. A condition of the marriage was that Charles would allow the
queen free exercise of her religion at Court. This was bound to
infuriate an anti-Catholic public, and by the time Charles called his
first parliament in June, 1625 the combination of religious fears and
financial mismanagement of the war provoked MPs into action.
Instead of granting Charles the right to collect Tunnage and
Poundage (customs duties) for life, as was customary, they limited the
right to one year only. This was not only an insult to the king, it
greatly increased his already serious financial problems.

Worse was to follow: the new parliament of 1626, infuriated by
Buckingham's inept handling of affairs, threatened to impeach him.
This would involve him being prosecuted by the House of Commons in
a trial held before the House of Lords, and could result in imprisonment, or worse. Charles dissolved parliament in order to protect his
friend. This early dissolution deprived Charles of supplies (the contemporary word for parliamentary taxation) and prevented a resolution of
the dispute over Tunnage and Poundage. Charles continued to collect
these duties without parliamentary approval. He also raised more
money by demanding forced loans; those who refused to pay were
imprisoned. In 1627 the Judges in the Five Knights Case established the
legality of this high-handed action, but this led parliament to present *A
Petition of Right* when it reassembled in 1628. This declared that the
imprisonment of men without proper cause shown was illegal, as was
the collection of taxes without parliamentary consent. MPs also
renewed their attacks on Buckingham, whose expedition to La Rochelle
in support of French Protestants in 1627 had ended in costly failure.

To protect his favourite, Charles prorogued parliament (suspended its sitting). In August 1628 Buckingham was assassinated, but

this did nothing to solve the underlying problems. Charles was furious at the attitude of parliament, whom he regarded as irresponsible and reluctant to contribute to the needs of the government, and he was both unable and unwilling to accept the need to account for his policies in the way that MPs wished. Although the parliament of 1628 did grant subsidies, he regarded their demand for accountability on the part of ministers, if not of the king himself, as too high a price to pay. His reaction to their criticisms, however, led him into actions that were barely legal, and certainly high-handed, raising fears that he had little respect for the rule of law. Charles's reaction to any opposition was always to interpret it as malicious – since he was sure of his conscience and motives, he could not understand how others could see matters in a different light, and he was inclined to view any opposing views as deliberate attacks on his authority. He therefore responded by asserting what he regarded as his rightful powers, regardless of circumstances.

When MPs' complaints were renewed in the next parliamentary session in 1629, the king decided to end such fruitless arguments by proroguing parliament once more. By now there was growing concern over his policies in the Church, as well as his attitude towards parliaments. However, when his message reached the Commons, angry MPs held the Speaker in his chair to prevent their dismissal while they passed *Three Resolutions*. In this act of open defiance they expressed their grievances over arbitrary imprisonment, the collection of taxes without parliamentary consent, and the changes being introduced in the Church. Infuriated by such behaviour, he dissolved parliament, arrested the ringleaders, and declared that he would have no more parliaments until his subjects should 'know his mind better'. He therefore set out to implement his preferred vision of good government in a period of personal rule.

ii) The Personal Rule, 1629–37

The characteristic of government under the personal rule, which opponents described as an 'Eleven Years Tyranny', was an attempt to establish order, hierarchy and uniformity across the British kingdoms. Nowhere was this more clearly demonstrated than in the Church. Charles favoured the minority, Arminian wing of Anglicans, who wished to restore traditional ceremonies and increase the authority of bishops and the clergy. In 1628 he had appointed one of this group, William Laud, as Bishop of London, and in 1633 he promoted him to the archbishopric of Canterbury, the highest position in the Church of England. Under Laud's leadership new ceremonies were introduced, altars were removed to the east end of churches and railed off from the laity, preaching was discouraged in favour of set prayers, and rules, old and new, were rigidly enforced. Puritans who, up to then, had got by with a token acceptance were now forced to obey or leave.

Essentially, the practical compromise with Puritan feeling that had been operated by James was shattered.

To make matters worse, these policies were conducted against a background of growing leniency towards Catholics. Recusancy laws which fined Catholics for not attending Church were enforced, possibly for the income that they produced but, under the patronage of the Queen, a Catholic party developed at Court (for example the Catholic Lord Weston was Lord Treasurer until his death in 1635), and in 1637 an envoy from the pope was publicly received and honoured by the King. Complaints against such policies led to harsh punishments – in 1637 three protesters, Burton, Bastwick and Prynne were publicly mutilated and imprisoned for writing and publishing attacks on the Queen and on Laud's policies. All three had their ears clipped, and Prynne was also branded on the face. The event was particularly shocking to contemporaries, since such brutal punishments were not normally applied to the gentry or professional classes except in extreme cases.

The other significant appointment made by Charles at this time was that of Sir Thomas Wentworth, who was created Lord Strafford and a member of the Privy Council in 1628. Strafford had participated in the attacks on Buckingham in the 1620s, and his acceptance of office (he became Lord President of the Council of the North in 1628 and Lord Deputy of Ireland in 1632) was regarded by many MPs as a betrayal. Strafford's complaints, however, had been motivated mainly by Buckingham's inefficiency, and this concern for efficient government characterised his work in both the North of England and in Ireland. The hand of central government was increasingly felt in the localities, more especially because of Charles's attempts to raise new revenue and secure financial independence from parliament. Monopolies were sold again and forest laws [special laws relating to areas of the country that were designated as royal forests] and feudal payments were revived.

Above all, however, it was the levying of Ship Money that brought the government close to success. This was an ancient and occasional tax, levied on ports and coastal towns to pay for naval defence. Charles levied the tax in 1634, and in 1635 extended it to inland areas. By 1636 it was clearly becoming a regular tax and unlike parliamentary taxes, the government set the amount required, without reference to formal assessments or limits. Challenged in the courts by John Hampden in 1637, it was declared legal although the judges were divided in their opinions. This was a serious blow to those who hoped to use parliament and the king's financial needs to restrain him, and in 1637–8 both John Pym and the Duke of Bedford, leaders of the Puritan faction, were considering emigration as a way out.

iii) Collapse and crisis, 1637–40

What changed the situation was the ill-fated attempt in 1637 to impose a revised English Prayer Book on the Church in Scotland. Charles was determined to create uniformity of government, and in particular of religion, in the three kingdoms (England/Wales, Ireland and Scotland) which he ruled as separate units. This was not unreasonable, and James had already taken steps in that direction. The English parliament had rejected his plans for Anglo-Scottish union in 1607, but he had encouraged Protestant settlement by both Scots and English in Ireland. By 1621 he had persuaded the Scots to accept bishops in the Scottish Church, but in the face of widespread opposition to further change, he had the sense to slow down. By nature and conviction, however, Charles lacked such caution. In 1637 the use of the Prayer Book in St. Giles Cathedral in Edinburgh sparked off a riot which turned to a widespread rebellion known, appropriately, as the Bishops' Wars.

In 1638, a Scottish assembly rejected both the prayer book and the bishops, and a National Covenant (agreement) was set up to defend the Presbyterian system. The Covenanters raised an army which defeated Charles in 1639 and forced him to sign the Treaty of Berwick. This allowed a Scottish synod (assembly of ministers) to decide on the organisation of the Church. They confirmed the decisions of 1638, rejecting the Prayer Book and abolishing bishops. It is possible that Charles had never intended the treaty to be more than a breathing space. In the event, such an open rejection of his policies made it certain that the treaty would not be adhered to. Moreover, he seems to have been blind to the impact of his actions in England as well as Scotland, and unaware of the extent of discontent that his policies had generated. In April 1640 he called an English parliament, believing that traditional anti-Scottish feeling would rally sufficient support to gain supplies.

He proved to be sadly mistaken. Opposition leaders were already in touch with the Scots, and insisted that their grievances be considered first. Charles angrily dismissed MPs (creating the nickname of the Short Parliament) and published new Canons (rules) for the Church, which embodied and enforced the changes made by Laud. At this point the Scots invaded England and besieged Newcastle. Charles called a Great Council of the nobility to meet at York, but his appeal for loans was met by the Twelve Peers Petition which requested him to call parliament. When the Scots insisted on a new truce (the Treaty of Ripon) in which Charles was committed to pay the costs of their army (£850 a day) it was clear that he no longer had any other option. On 3 November 1640 the parliament that was to be known as the Long Parliament assembled at Westminster. It would not be formally dissolved until 1660.

Summary Diagram

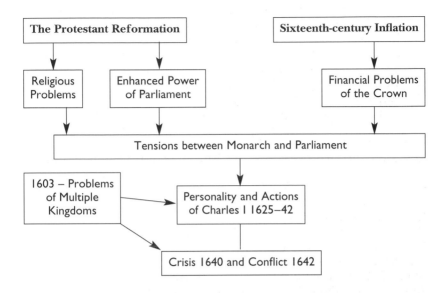

The Protestant Reformation → Religious Problems, Enhanced Power of Parliament

Sixteenth-century Inflation → Financial Problems of the Crown

Tensions between Monarch and Parliament

1603 – Problems of Multiple Kingdoms → Personality and Actions of Charles I 1625–42

Crisis 1640 and Conflict 1642

Working on Chapter I

You do not need to make detailed notes on this chapter, as it is mainly intended to be an outline, enabling you to trace the roots of the crisis in the sixteenth century and its development through the reigns of James I and Charles I. However, it would be helpful for you to establish a clear understanding of that process, by using the information contained in it to complete the tasks below.

Task I. The Significance of the Reformation

Using the information provided, construct a spider diagram to show the different effects of the Reformation on the political system and the nature of the ruling class in England. You should then describe as fully as you can how the Reformation made parliament a more important political institution. Consider social and economic changes as well as the political role of parliaments, and explain fully the implications of each aspect that you select. The best descriptions will also try to bring out the links between these different aspects, to explain their overall effect.

Events like the Reformation are often referred to as a *turning-point* in history, because they affect long term developments as well as the people at the time. When you are studying developments over a long period of time, it is important not to collect too much detail about short periods and individual events, because that makes it difficult to gain a clear picture of the overall process. However, you do need some detail about events that were particularly significant, so that if you have to write a thematic account of the period [as you will have to in all of the present A level courses], you will be able to draw out and explain their significance. The secret of a good thematic account is the ability to select valid turning-points, accelerators, or barriers to development, and to be able to link them up by bringing out their significance to create an overall explanation of change as an ongoing process. A good way of starting this is to construct a timeline.

To start with, you should draw a line across the centre of the page, and mark on to it the time span that you need to cover, equally divided into decades, so that you have established a time framework. You can then place your events onto it, at the appropriate points. If you draw up a timeline on a single sheet of A4 paper [landscape width], you will not be able to fit in all of the events that you read about, which means that you must *select* particular events according to their significance. This will make you think about the events as the starting point for your account, and later you can think about how to link them up.

Task 2. Re-read chapter 1, and draw up separate timelines to show:

The development of parliamentary power in England, 1500–1640.
Changes in religion in England, 1500–1640

The value of completing two timelines together is that you will have to think carefully about the selection of events for inclusion according to the different titles – you need to think about what each is designed to show. Some events will probably appear on both, others on only one.

When you have completed your timelines, work with other students to compare and discuss your selections of events. You must be able to explain why you chose to include your selection, and you must make a note of their ideas. You should find that the events that you have all included are the most important, and that other choices vary according to your different opinions about the overall pattern of the development. When you have completed this task, you should use all the ideas that you have developed to write a brief account of how the powers of parliament, and/or religious ideas and attitudes changed between 1500 and 1640.

Further Reading

Because this introductory chapter covers a very long period in outline, you may want to know more about the events covered. For advice on books and other resources, see the Further Reading section on p. 153.

2 From Crisis to Conflict, 1640–2

POINTS TO CONSIDER

Chapter 1 explained why Charles I was facing a crisis in 1640, but this does not necessarily explain why King and Parliament went to war in 1642. The crisis certainly made war possible, but by no means inevitable, and at the time no-one would have expected that to be the end result. Both King and Parliament assumed that a settlement could be negotiated. In order to understand why war broke out in 1642 it is necessary to explain why the attempt to negotiate a settlement failed. Since neither side intended to start an armed conflict, it is likely that the failure arose from errors and misjudgements. The opposition sought to pressurise the King to accept restrictions on his power, but this process led to divisions within parliament and the growth of fear and mistrust, so that eventually both sides felt obliged to take up arms. As you work through this chapter you should try to trace the process of division and identify the key turning-points that brought about such fear and mistrust.

KEY DATES

1640	November	The Long Parliament assembled.
1641	February	Triennial Act passed.
	May	Execution of Strafford.
	June	Bishops' Exclusion Bill rejected by the Lords.
		Root and Branch Bill failed.
		Presentation of the Ten Propositions.
	July	Prerogative Courts abolished.
	August	Ship Money was declared illegal.
		The Parliamentary session ended and King Charles left for Scotland.
	October	Outbreak of rebellion in Ireland.
	November	King returned from Scotland and presented with the Grand Remonstrance.
	December	Militia Bill introduced, Grand Remonstrance published. Parliament clearly divided into two factions.
1642	January	Attempt by Charles to arrest parliamentary leaders led to riots in London, King Charles left for York.
	February	Militia Ordinance passed, Bishops excluded from the House of Lords.
1642	June	Nineteen Propositions presented and rejected.
	August	King Charles raised his standard at Nottingham and called for volunteers.

1 Introduction

> **KEY ISSUE** Why did an unexpected and unwanted war break out?

The Civil War was an enormous shock and upheaval for those involved in it, and it is important not to underestimate the fear and horror with which such an event would be regarded. Since the late fifteenth century England had enjoyed 150 years of internal peace, but contemporaries were well aware of the effects of civil war on France in the last decades of the sixteenth century and on Germany since 1618. The English Civil Wars lasted for more than six years (with a break of twelve months) and, if the perspective is widened to Britain as a whole, bloodshed continued from the Bishops' Wars of 1639–40 to the final defeat of Charles II at Worcester in 1651. As a proportion of the total population, more men were involved and more died than during the Great War of 1914–18. In addition, the wars were fought on British soil with all the resulting destruction of property, dislocation of trade, and burden of incessant taxation. In short, civil war was nasty, brutish and destructive, and although contemporaries could not foresee the full horror of what lay ahead, many would have had some idea.

It is important, therefore, to avoid any assumption that England slipped easily into war, or that such an outcome could be seriously contemplated when parliament met in 1640. 'Great expectance there is of a happy parliament, where the subject may have a total redress of all his grievances' wrote the Yorkshire MP, Sir Henry Slingsby, in his diary in November 1640. Eighteen months later, in the summer of 1642, the MP Bulstrode Whitelock reflected sadly that 'we have slid into the beginnings of a civil war by one unexpected accident after another ... So that we scarcely know how we have come this far; but from paper combats ... we are now come to the question of raising forces.' While Slingsby fought for the king, Whitelocke supported parliament throughout the war.

It is clear that in 1640 grievances against the king's recent policies were widespread; according to Slingsby, the Commons 'apply themselves to question all delinquents, all those who bought and set up monopolies, those who levied ship money, and such judges as gave it for law'.

This is confirmed by Richard Baxter, a Puritan minister who was present in London and described the mood of the Commons:

1   They made many long and vehement speeches against the ship money, and against the judges that gave their judgement for it, and against the Et Cetera oath [a promise to obey all the new rules of the Church] and the Bishops and Convocation that were the formers of it; but especially
5   against the Lord Thomas Wentworth, Lord Deputy of Ireland, and Dr Laud, Archbishop of Canterbury, as evil counsellors, the cause of all ...

It is apparent from his comments that, like Whitelocke and Baxter, Slingsby supported the widespread demand for redress of grievances. However, the fact that he later fought for the King suggests that grievances alone do not explain why men took up arms against their king, and it cannot be assumed, therefore, that the crisis of 1640 would lead automatically to armed conflict. Thus the long-term problems and accumulation of grievances outlined in Chapter 1 may provide the necessary precondition for the war, but do not explain the outbreak of war itself. Not all of those who complained in 1640 were willing to take up arms against the king in 1642. Had they been prepared to do so, there could have been no civil war, for the king would have been unable to raise an army. It was precisely because some of those who disapproved of his actions up to 1640 were, in the end, prepared to defend him and his right to govern, that a royalist 'side' emerged, and until this happened there was no question of military conflict. Even then, the existence of two 'sides' did not ensure that the crisis would come to a military conclusion, or even a conclusion at all at this particular time. A similar crisis in 1628–9 had been overcome by the king dissolving parliament and governing without reference to that body, but in 1640–1, parliament was not dissolved, and in 1642 the result was not government without parliament, but war.

There are, therefore, a number of questions to be addressed in considering how and why the crisis of 1640 ended in civil war rather than settlement as expected by Slingsby and others like him.

- First, if we begin by asking what Charles's critics wanted in 1640, i.e. what grievances they wanted to address, we can define the underlying issues and aims for which they fought.
- Secondly, we need to consider why Charles was unwilling or unable to provide the land of settlement that they wanted, and why, given his desperate situation, he felt able to reject some of their demands.
- Thirdly, we have to explain why their apparently solid support began to crumble, why, ultimately, two parties emerged, and what issues caused men of similar class, status and outlook to choose different sides.
- Finally it is necessary to explain why these parties felt compelled to resolve their differences quickly and decisively, by force if required, rather than to allow the situation to continue or to seek a long-term solution.

To offer an adequate explanation of why the crisis of 1640 became the war of 1642, we need to address all of these issues. The fact that the evidence available to historians is so often uncertain and inconclusive makes this a difficult task. Aims and intentions must be inferred from actions that can be misunderstood, or that were deliberately devised to be misleading, and from statements that may or may not be acceptable at face value. Attitudes, values and the impact of events can be interpreted from a range of sources, but the extent to which these may be applied to any individual inevitably varies. Herein, of course, lies one of the major causes of disagreements between historians.

2 From Crisis to Conflict

a) Actions and Intentions, November 1640–May 1641

> **KEY ISSUES** What were the objectives and intentions of the King and opposition in the autumn of 1640? What actions did they take to pursue those objectives? Why did they expect to be successful?

i) The King

Whatever Slingsby may have expected, there is little to suggest that redress of grievances was part of the king's agenda in November 1640. His ill-advised attempt to impose an adapted English Prayer Book on Scotland in 1637 had provoked his northern kingdom to rebellion, and he had found himself unable to raise and maintain effective forces from an English population which was almost equally discontented. As a result, he had been forced to conclude a treaty at Berwick in June 1639. The king's character and attitudes are clearly shown in the events that followed. Far from accepting the defeat of his religious policy, Charles had set about obtaining the means to renew the war. Unable to raise enough revenue from existing sources, he had summoned parliament in April 1640, and dissolved it in less than a month rather than accept its demand for redress of grievances. Still oblivious to the necessity of compromise, he had raised new forces to meet a Scottish invasion. Defeated, and with negotiations under way at Ripon, Charles had tried the expedient of calling a Great Council [of the nobility] to meet him at York. Only the refusal of the Lords to support him unless he recalled parliament had finally forced him to accept the necessity of summoning and dealing with that body. When the Treaty of Ripon left the Scots in England and Charles bound to pay them £850 a day for their trouble, it had became clear that some concessions would have to be made. However, his behaviour in November revealed just how few and limited he intended those concessions to be.

When he opened the session of parliament on 3 November, Charles arrived at Westminster by river barge. This avoided the normal public procession and signalled his intention to complete the necessary business of obtaining parliamentary subsidies with as few concessions as possible. The opposition leaders had few illusions on the matter. John Pym's exhortation to the Scottish army around Newcastle to 'sit tight' revealed his awareness that only their presence in England, and the king's consequent need for money, had provided this opportunity to air the grievances that had accumulated since the bitter dissolution of 1629. Charles's experience of parliaments between 1625 and 1629, and their reluctance to accept responsibility for the necessary expenses of government, had given him little reason to view MPs as positive and reliable partners. The fact was that he had summoned this parliament out of necessity and as a last resort.

The significance of Charles's actions at this point was not that he behaved illegally or unconstitutionally, which he did not, but that he showed an inflexible perception of his own role as king and a dangerous absence of political skill. Charles did not doubt for one moment that it was his right to govern according to his conscience in both Church and state, across all of his kingdoms. Control of the Church was an essential part of government, and quite apart from his own deep belief in the validity of the Anglican faith, there were difficulties in allowing Presbyterianism in Scotland while attacking Presbyterians in England. As a number of historians have suggested in drawing attention to the problems of governing multiple kingdoms, it was not unreasonable in itself to seek to establish clear and uniform procedures throughout all three realms. In Charles's eyes, therefore, any opposition or resistance to his commands must be both unjustified and malicious.

Armoured by his own convictions – not only his belief in the rightness of Laudian Anglicanism but also his sense of his own, God-given rights and duties as king – Charles was incapable of seeing and understanding the fears and concerns of others. Since he had no intention of restoring Catholicism, nor of governing without reference to law unless he was forced to do so, he could not comprehend the existence of fears about Catholic tyranny. Hence he was also incapable of genuine compromise, since he did not understand the concerns and fears that required it. What was perhaps even more serious in political terms was that he also lacked the confidence and flexibility to recognise when it would be advantageous to appear to compromise, if only temporarily. Because he believed his position to be right, Charles failed to recognise when circumstances required him to shift it. When finally forced to make concessions, for example in summoning this new parliament in November 1640, he did so with such obvious reluctance as to rob them of their worth and raise doubts about how far he could be trusted to keep whatever promises he made.

ii) The Parliamentary Opposition

Unlike Slingsby, the opposition leadership was well aware of Charles's character and had considerable experience of his methods. Three of them – John Pym, Sir Arthur Haselrig and Denzil Holles – had played a significant part in the parliamentary crisis of 1628–9 and had seen those who were responsible for the Three Resolutions of 1629 end in the Tower of London, where one, Sir John Eliot, died after two years of imprisonment. For almost a decade they had been powerless to respond, but throughout the Scottish crisis of 1637–40 they had been in touch with the Scots, and it was this co-ordinated pressure that had led to the calling of parliament and the opportunity to present grievances. Now the same kind of pressure would be required to ensure that those grievances were adequately redressed, and to build in safeguards for the future. In particular, the feelings of the nation within and outside parliament would have to be roused, and maintained at a pitch where Charles would be forced by necessity, and even fear, to agree to measures that he would never accept voluntarily. According to Clarendon this strategy was clearly defined, at least in the mind of Pym, from the first meeting of the Long Parliament. He described a chance meeting with Pym in early November.

1   Mr Hyde [as Clarendon then was] met Mr Pym in Westminster Hall some days before the parliament, and conferring together upon the state of affairs, Pym told him ... that they must now be of another temper than they were the last parliament [in April 1640]; ... that
5   they had now an opportunity to make their country happy, by removing all grievances, and pulling up the causes of them by the roots, if all men would do their duties. Which suggested that the warmest and boldest counsel would find a much better reception than those of a more temperate nature; which happened accordingly.

The opposition campaign was well organised. Speeches in the House of Commons were supported by a flood of petitions laying out complaints against unparliamentary taxation (especially Ship Money), the fines levied by the Star Chamber and other prerogative courts, changes in the Church, and the general 'countenancing of Popery' and 'discountenancing' of 'forward men in our religion', as Pym described the Puritan party. The focus of complaint was fixed upon the 'evil counsellors' who were to be held responsible, and whose fate would serve as a warning to others as well as depriving the king of his most effective servants. On 10 November the impeachment of Strafford was moved in the Commons and eight days later Archbishop Laud was also impeached. On 11 December the Root and Branch Petition for the reform of the Church was presented to the Commons, so that by the end of the year, within two months of parliament meeting, the main issues had been laid out and the first steps of remedial action could now be taken.

The first priority was the protection of parliament itself, and the *Triennial Act*, ensuring that parliaments would sit at least every three years, was presented to the king in February 1641. Complaining that 'you have taken the government almost to pieces and, I may say, it is almost off the hinges', Charles reluctantly gave his assent to the Act. By doing so he signalled that he could be pressured into making concessions, thereby confirming the opposition in their chosen strategy. When they found in February and March that they lacked suffi-

THE EARL OF CLARENDON

-Profile-

The Earl of Clarendon provides one of the most important sources of evidence about the period, in his *History of the Great Rebellion,* and was also an active and important politician. Born Edward Hyde, a Wiltshire landowner, he trained as a common lawyer and was elected MP for Saltash in Cornwall in 1640. In the early months of the Long Parliament he shared the opposition's concern with grievances, but not their religious fears. By the summer of 1641 he had become convinced that they were pushing a radical agenda in both Church and state, and began to organise a moderate royalist faction to support a compromise settlement. In 1642 he gave his support to the King and acted as a royal adviser throughout the war, despite often becoming frustrated with the King's more extreme tendencies and associates. In 1646 he went into exile with the young Prince Charles, and served him as chief adviser both before and after his restoration in 1660, when he was rewarded with a title and a seat in the House of Lords. His account of events is often balanced and objective, although undoubtedly coloured by his royalist sympathies, his personal relationships, and his knowledge of how matters finally turned out.

cient evidence and strength to impeach Strafford successfully, they sought to use the king's weakness once more. In April a Bill for Strafford's Attainder was introduced into the House of Commons. An Attainder required that parliament should pass a law to declare Strafford guilty of treason, and would need the King's consent. Attainders had been used by medieval kings to deal with over-mighty nobles, but since they provided no trial or chance for the accused to defend themselves, there were many who had reservations about such a strategy. However, Strafford's unpopularity, and his undoubted skill and determination made him a dangerous opponent, and the opposition leaders could not afford to leave him in a position of power.

Both moral and physical persuasion was used to silence the doubters. As the crucial vote approached there were noisy scenes in London as the opposition and their allies organised a petition calling for Strafford's death; when the vote was taken in the Commons on 21 April only 59 MPs were prepared to vote against the Bill, although almost one third of the House had found it wise to be absent. Further intimidation ensued when the Bill moved to the House of Lords. Crowds gathered outside the House and those known to have opposed the Attainder were jostled and threatened – the result was that when a vote was taken, only 46 Lords were present, with only 11 voting against. Finally, when the king refused his assent, as he had promised Strafford he would, the mobs invaded Whitehall itself and the threat to the queen and his children was sufficient to destroy his resistance. On 9 May Charles signed away the life of his most effective minister, and in a telling comment written on the day of Strafford's execution, Laud described him as a prince who 'knew not how to be, or to be made, great'.

iii) The King's Failure

These events emphasise the weakness of Charles's strategy in calling the Long Parliament. If he planned to gain financial support at the cost of a few concessions he had clearly misjudged the situation and, finding himself hemmed in, had no choice but to make concessions where necessary, in order to buy time in which to find alternatives. These alternatives were not necessarily consistent. In April he flirted with the idea of a military solution when a group of army officers led by Sir John Ashburnham concocted a plot to release Strafford from the Tower, arrest the opposition leaders, and disperse parliament. Within the same month Charles also considered buying off the opposition leadership by offering them power and positions in government. The suggestion came from the Earl of Bedford, Pym's patron and ally, that Charles should appoint them to office, with Pym being named as Chancellor of the Exchequer. Whether anything could have come of this plan is uncertain – it was forestalled by Bedford's untimely death in early May. What is clear is that Charles was desperately seeking a way out of his difficulties and, as so often, his willingness to consider contradictory methods robbed him of success in any one of them. As a reigning monarch carrying responsibility for government he had every right to consider a range of strategies, but his inconsistencies did help to build up a politically dangerous lack of trust. It is not clear how far he was involved in the army plot, but when it was revealed by Pym in early May it did the king enormous damage and greatly increased the distrust and suspicion with which he was regarded. The fact that Ashburnham kept his seat on the Privy Council far outweighed any denials that Charles had known or approved of the plan.

His intentions and and the errors that he made are relatively easy to define and analyse, since this involves the study of the actions and beliefs of one man. While different historians may emphasise different aspects of Charles's character and behaviour, and attribute different significance to these in comparison with other factors that influenced the outcome of events, there is broad agreement about what Charles wanted to achieve and why he failed to achieve it. Far more difficult to distinguish, and hence a matter of greater and more contentious debate, is the nature and intentions of the 'opposition' and its leaders.

b) The Nature of the Opposition

> **KEY ISSUES** Why did Charles face such organised and
> determined opposition? What were the opposition leaders trying
> to achieve?

The modern concept of a parliamentary opposition, seeking to change government policy in a legitimate and acceptable way, was unknown in the seventeenth century. Government belonged to the king, and the ministers and officers who carried out its executive functions were his servants, appointed and dismissed by him according to his own choices and desires. The role of parliament was three-fold – to inform the king of his subjects' needs and desires through the medium of petitioning, to pass such laws as were necessary for government to function, and to provide money through taxation for occasional and exceptional expenses. The concept of king-in-parliament, which underpinned the seventeenth-century constitution, related more to the supremacy of law than to any idea that parliament had a separate or restraining power on the king's choice of policy or ministers. The king made the law, but the laws that he made **in** parliaments could only be changed in a parliament and with the consent of both Lords and Commons. Such laws could not be ignored or removed by the king alone – hence the concept of king-in-parliament as the highest authority offered subjects some legal protection against arbitrary actions by the king.

It did not, however, imply that parliament, acting alone, could challenge the king's decisions. The law made by the king through the institution of parliament was the highest law of the land made by king-in-parliament, but it was still initiated, designed and devised by the king (or his chosen servants) and parliament's function in the process was legal and constitutional rather than political. The ancient constitution, to which Pym and his associates so often referred in their attempts to restrict Charles, was at most a system of customary law, supported by a number of specific charters by which kings had agreed to grant and maintain certain rights and privileges, or 'liberties', in carrying out their function of governing. Powerful as was its appeal, the ancient constitution did not imply government by king and parliament as separate partners, and certainly had no place for a permanent, political opposition. Yet it is clear that in 1640 Charles was faced with a well-organised parliamentary group, determined to undo the work of his chosen ministers and force him to adopt both new men and new policies.

i) Historians' Interpretations and Debates: Where did the 'opposition' party come from?

The traditional explanation for this has been that the wealth and confidence of the House of Commons had greatly increased over the previous century and that the use made of parliament in the Reformation and the series of religious and political settlements that followed had given the institution a new status. The 'opposition' was portrayed as a coherent group dedicated to reforming the system of government. Other theories have suggested that the opposition was motivated by economic grievances, or by a resentment of a dominant and centralising Court. Whatever the motivation, these arguments all presented a picture of a numerous, united and coherent opposition party.

Recent research suggests that all such explanations involve a measure of over-simplification in seeking to explain the causes of the Civil War within a single theme. As Conrad Russell wrote in the Introduction to his *Origins of the Civil War*, 'it has become painfully clear that it is impossible to interpret the Civil War as the clash of two clearly differentiated social groups or classes ... Nor are we trying to find causes for a conflict between a court and a country, or a government and an opposition'. Like most recent writers on the subject, he has argued against the traditional picture of a numerous opposition, united in a single purpose, and challenging an oppressive monarch for political power. Nevertheless, it is clear that Charles was dealing with something more than local or individual resentments, however numerous. Russell himself described an opposition leadership, which he labelled 'Pym's Junto', and it is inconceivable that such a group could have managed the parliamentary programme of 1640–1 without a large, if inconsistent, measure of support among MPs. Some historians, notably John Adamson who has suggested that the Civil Wars began as a traditional 'baronial revolt', explain much of their organisation as the work of an aristocratic faction who were seeking power for themselves. [This view is put forward in C. Jones ed. *A Pillar of the Constitution*, pp. 29–31.] Even if the claim is accepted, however, it does not explain the support that they received, nor what MPs thought they were achieving by their votes. While it has been generally agreed that the challenge to the authority of the King in 1640–2 cannot be related to a single overriding issue, the precise size, intentions and objectives of the 'opposition' remain a matter of some debate.

ii) The Significance of the Debate: Why does it matter?

The importance of this debate is that it implies quite different explanations, not only of why a war broke out, but also of what that war meant. If the opposition was widespread, reflecting deeply held beliefs and principles, then historians can speak plausibly of 'revolution' in English government, or at least of deep-seated and serious problems underlying the crisis. This does not mean that the opposition leaders were conscious revolutionaries – indeed most historians would accept the arguments of Russell and others that the opposition were mounting a defensive campaign against a king whom they thought was seeking to change traditional relationships in government. What was potentially revolutionary was their willingness to change the constitution in order to resist him. If, however, the opposition amounted to little more than an aristocratic conspiracy, then the war must be seen as an act of rebellion arising from their failure to control the process that they had started. In either case, the war itself could be seen as accidental, or at least unintended. What is at issue is whether the aims of the opposition were to reform, or merely to take control of, the existing system of government.

At first sight, then, we are faced with conflicting and incompatible interpretations, which have a considerable bearing on the central issue of why war broke out in 1642, and on the events that followed in the next two decades. As we know, historical events are rarely to be explained by any single factor, deriving instead from the interaction of a number of issues, and while there continues to be room and cause for debate, the different interpretations can, on closer examination, be largely reconciled. It may well be the case, for example, that a group of opposition peers sought to use the anger of the Commons to attain power for themselves, and that influential MPs were content to accept their leadership. Indeed, given the structure of seventeenth-century society, it would be surprising if this did not occur. This does not mean that the causes of that anger were not genuine and significant, nor that the leaders, aristocratic or otherwise, did not share the beliefs and concerns that lay behind it. Power for 'themselves' may well also mean power to carry out policies that they believed to be right for society and religion.

Nor is it necessary to find a single, all-embracing issue in order to explain the apparent unity achieved by those seeking to rally and direct the resentment that existed. A man whose main concern was religion might have no difficulty in sympathising with those who disliked the extension of central power over local government, if that power was seen as the source of both the political and religious problems. The opponents of Laud and the enemies of Strafford had much in common, and might well be expected to make common cause in the right conditions. According to Richard Baxter, who observed the MPs at the time, it was precisely a mixture of grievances of this kind that created widespread discontent in 1640 and in that sense it was Charles himself who laid the basis of opposition support. His financial policies, religious reforms, use of the prerogative courts, and extension of central power in all his three kingdoms gave rise to a range of grievances that affected most men in one way or another and created the potential for resistance. What made his position so dangerous was the existence of leaders whose political skills and influence enabled them to hold the shifting mass together, and whose own political or religious objectives may have gone beyond those that they publicly expressed.

iii) Assessment – The Nature and Origins of the Opposition: Who were the 'opposition' and what did they want?

It is, therefore, possible to resolve a number of apparent conflicts of interpretation and draw some broad conclusions concerning the nature of the 'opposition' and their part in the outbreak of war. It can be said, for example, that there existed within the House of Commons in 1640 a coherent opposition group – Conrad Russell's 'Pym's junto' – which was organised, employed clearly defined tactics, and had specific aims. There is room for debate about how extensively the group was organised and about the role of the lords with whom it was closely associated, but there is no doubt that its origins as a group can be traced back to the political crises of the 1620s. By 1640 its centre was John Pym, a skilful political tactician who had first entered parliament in 1620. He had participated in the Commons' Protestation (against James's refusal to allow them to debate foreign policy) of 1621 and in the attack on the king's favourite, the Duke of Buckingham. Resentment of the duke's power and anger at his incompetence in the direction of foreign policy had brought together a group of lords and MPs [the Earl of Warwick, Lord Saye and Sele, and Sir John Eliot among them] who continued to oppose Charles's high-handedness after his favourite had been assassinated. They organised the Petition of Right in 1628 and a year later we find these names joined with others – Holles, Valentine, Hampden and Pym – in the crisis that produced the *Three Resolutions* of 1629. The crises of the 1620s, therefore, established personal friendships and contacts among these men and also provided a measure of political and parliamentary experience, which was used to good effect in 1640.

What they had in common was a belief that the law of the land was binding on the king as well as his subjects and a religious outlook that was Puritan, or at least strongly anti-Catholic. In both areas, Charles's policies offended and frightened them and his actions in 1629, and after, increased their fears. The dissolution of parliament and the king's obvious reluctance to call another, the attempt to gain financial independence in the 1630s, and, above all, Arminianism in the Church and Catholic influence at Court, convinced those who were already suspicious of Charles that he sought to establish a continental-style and possibly Catholic, absolutism. It is difficult to trace their activities in the eleven-year absence of parliament between 1629 and 1640, but there is evidence of continuing contact of some kind. Pym and Bedford were both directors of the Providence Island Company, while Hampden's initiation of the Ship Money test case in 1637 was certainly not the act of a man working alone. These links are not sufficient to constitute a political organisation, but they did make it easier for plans and strategies to be evolved when the need and opportunity arose. There is little doubt that after the outbreak of rebellion in Scotland in 1638, contacts were established between the Scottish Covenanters and Pym's associates in England, notably through Nathaniel Fiennes, son and heir of Lord Saye and Sele (a title that often confuses as it seems to refer to more than one man – but it is a single title).

The experience of the Short Parliament in 1640 finalised the formation of a group, led in the Commons by Pym, who played an active role in preventing the granting of supplies. It was probably at this time that they began to develop both their organisation and their strategy. When Charles ordered the arrest of Lords Warwick, Brooke, and Saye and Sele (along with leading members of the Commons) after the dissolution of the Short Parliament, he was indicating those whom he believed to be the leaders of a faction, which is how he would have regarded them. This also indicates the dangers faced by those who organised political opposition to a king. The weeks that followed the opening of the Long Parliament revealed the extent and effectiveness of this opposition group. The main forum was the House of Commons, although contact and consultation with the opposition lords was clearly maintained. Pym's proposal of a Committee to consider the nation's grievances provided a powerful weapon against pressure and manipulation by the Court and care was taken to secure control of this and other important committees.

Opposition strategy was gradually revealed in the series of impeachments and bills proposed by different members of the group in the winter of 1640–1. Proceedings in parliament were supported by outside pressure and contacts – the petitions and demonstrations in London that accompanied major debates and votes such as those involved in the attainder of Strafford were undoubtedly organised and orchestrated to achieve maximum effect. Contacts with the Scots had already reached the point of treason. In short, Charles had to deal with an organised opposition that was skilled in political tactics. Although this organised core was small in numbers, it was able to direct and manipulate the anger of the parliament and nation for its own political purposes. What remains a matter of debate is the nature and extent of those purposes – what, in fact, the opposition was trying to achieve.

The leaders claimed to be trying merely to restore the balance of the constitution and the Protestant Church in order to protect the political and religious 'liberties'. These, they argued, had been undermined by the activities of 'evil counsellors' who had come between the king and his people. However, it is impossible to accept these stated purposes entirely at face value. The attack on Strafford and Laud, for example, portrayed the two men as the source of a conspiracy whose purpose was the destruction of English 'liberties', and treated the king as their innocent victim. But it is inconceivable, given their previous experience of him, that they did not see Charles I as the real source of their difficulties. It was just that the conventions of the time and the need to carry the support of the less sophisticated backbenchers made it impossible to attack the king directly. By concentrating attention on an unpopular minister like Strafford, Pym was able to rally the support of future royalists like Digby and Slingsby for a tactic which, in practice, undermined the king's free choice of advisers. The fact was that the opposition did not trust Charles and was seeking to bind him for the future. Given the number of lawyers in the opposition ranks, they were surely aware of the extent to which legislation such as the *Triennial Act* was adding to the powers of parliament and reducing those of the king, thereby changing, rather than restoring, the constitutional balance. Thus, interpreting their actions in the light of political attitudes and pressures of the time, it becomes necessary at the very least to redefine the opposition's aims as a desire to restore the balance of the constitution and the Protestant Church by depriving the king of the means to destroy it – his chosen advisers and the free exercise of his powers.

In practical terms, this meant new restrictions on the king's prerogative and an extension of the powers of parliament. And while there is no evidence to suggest that they were trying to achieve this for its own sake, it was a necessity that a man like Pym could happily accept. Nevertheless, he was on dangerous ground. Although widespread resentment of Charles's policies had built up during the absence of parliament, most MPs sought no more than the redress of grievances through the traditional channels, such as parliamentary petitions. They were realistic enough to know that Charles might have to be pressured into granting concessions, but changes in the constitution or in the king's governing functions were looked upon as dangerous innovations [new ideas]. In political terms, Pym's priority had to be to present the necessity of change in such a way as to carry the more naïve, or the more conservative, backbenchers with him.

However, one question that remains is the extent to which personal ambition influenced and motivated the opposition leadership in their plans. Clarendon and other royalists had no doubt that this was a major factor, and the fact that Pym, the Earl of Bedford and the lawyer, Oliver St John had worked out a plan to reorganise royal finances suggests that the king's proposal in May 1641 that they accept government office, was neither unexpected nor unwelcome. What is crucial in assessing the nature of the opposition is to decide whether this ambition constituted their primary motive, and the available evidence suggests that it was not. Bedford was a man born to political life by virtue of his title and position and Pym was an astute and experienced politician, but both appear to have held strong and sincere religious beliefs, to the point of considering emigration in 1637–8 rather than accept the reforms instituted by Laud. In that context, a willingness to accept office in the only form of government that they knew is as indicative of a desire to serve their cause as it is evidence of any greed for personal power. Government lay with the king, and only by gaining positions in the king's service could they establish a government that they, and others, could trust. Whether or not they could have succeeded in restraining or influencing Charles is quite another matter, but in the spring of 1641 both Bedford and Pym may reasonably have believed that this represented the only possible route to the settlement they desired.

In conclusion, therefore, it can be suggested that the 'opposition' to Charles and his government consisted of a small, organised and coherent group of parliamentarians (both in the Lords and the Commons) who were able to orchestrate and channel the widespread desire for redress of grievances in both Church and state towards the constitutional change which they believed necessary. They were capable of planning and carrying out a parliamentary programme and they intended to use their political and financial powers to force the king to adopt new policies and advisers, and to establish the future security of their parliament, their religion, their 'liberties' and themselves. In pursuit of these goals they were willing to use propaganda, persuasion, manipulation and intimidation. Until the execution of Strafford in May 1641, their story is one of remarkable success.

c) The First Turning-point: The Death of Strafford

> **KEY ISSUES** In what ways did Strafford's death affect the relationships between members of the parliament and the king? Why was this so significant?

The execution of Strafford marks a crucial stage in the shift from crisis to conflict. It appeared that if the king could be induced by pressure to break his word publicly and sacrifice the life of his most effective minister and a loyal servant, then there was little that could not be gained if the right kind of pressure could be maintained. Thus the opposition leaders were confirmed in their strategy and the pattern of changes to be forced upon a reluctant monarch was set for the spring and summer of 1641. In May, after Pym revealed that an Army Plot had been suggested to save Strafford and dissolve parliament by force, an *Act against the Dissolution of this Parliament without its own Consent* was passed, depriving Charles of the right to dissolve this parliament. In July the king accepted the abolition of the prerogative courts of Star Chamber and High Commission, and in August Ship Money was declared illegal. In each of these cases Charles accepted a significant reduction of his own power and independence.

At the same time, however, the game had become more dangerous. In order to remove Strafford the opposition had been forced to use the device of attainder and to threaten and humiliate the king. Any monarch would have felt justified in punishing those responsible when he had the opportunity, and it is not surprising that Charles considered the use of force to solve his problems. The army plot revealed in May provided clear evidence of his willingness to do so. It was reinforced by the queen's advice to call on her brother, the King of France, for money and arms. By the end of May 1641 there can have been little doubt in the minds of Pym and his associates that if their pressure should falter and their campaign to restrict the king's powers fail, they would pay with their fortunes and probably with their lives. According to Conrad Russell, 'an acceptable settlement, meaning one which would have left both Charles and Pym's Junto confident that they would be alive and at liberty in twelve months' time, had become remote by March 1641, and became a total impossibility between 3 and 12 May 1641' (*Causes of the English Civil War*, p. 213). This did not mean that civil war became inevitable at that date – a solution of some kind could still have been forced upon one party by the other – but it is unlikely that a settlement could have been reached to which both would willingly agree.

If this is the case, it is perhaps necessary to ask why the opposition adopted such a high-risk strategy. Russell's explanation is that their Scottish allies required Strafford's death as a condition of continuing support. Whether or not this was the case – the evidence is not conclusive – the junto had plenty of reason to fear Strafford's determination and effectiveness as a minister, and it is probably the case that, had Charles listened to his advice more often in the years before 1640, their present opportunity to reverse or restrict his policies would not have existed. The future royalist, Lord Digby, declared him to be 'the most dangerous minister, the most insupportable to free subjects, that can be charactered'. The likelihood is that genuine fear of Strafford's abilities as well as the underlying strategy of attacking the king through his servants would have made his death a necessity, with or without Scottish pressure.

Strafford's execution and the means of attaining it, therefore, made a genuine settlement of differences impossible. The opposition had gone too far ever to retract, and both they and the king knew it. Even if Charles should agree to a compromise, the opposition leadership would not dare to trust his word. Hence the only acceptable settlement for Pym and his associates would either be one in which the king's power was so limited as to render him unable to punish them, or one in which parliament's powers were sufficient to protect them. For their own safety, and because they could not, and did not, trust the king to uphold concessions that had been forced from him, they could not afford to be content with the political and constitutional gains which had been made by the early summer of 1641. They had already succeeded in removing the abuses of the past, and their apparent authors, but to rest secure they also had to ensure that they could not reappear. Since the real, but politically untouchable, author of the problem was the king himself, only by binding and limiting his powers could they ensure future security. By executing Strafford and impeaching Laud the opposition had deprived the king, and themselves, of convenient scapegoats. They were therefore forced openly to attack the powers of the king, in a way that some of their own supporters might well find unacceptable.

d) The Loss of Parliamentary Unity, May 1641–January 1642

KEY ISSUES Why did the apparent unity of parliament begin to disappear? What issues divided MPs and their supporters?

i) Unity and its Problems

The opposition leaders' difficulties lay in the interaction of three factors. In the first place, they were now undeniably engaged in a power struggle with the king that they could not afford to lose. Secondly, any progress in this struggle would involve limiting the king's powers and hence encroaching on his valid and accepted prerogatives. Thirdly, and here lay the core of their problem, they could only succeed in doing this by maintaining the unity of parliament, or at least of the Commons. This meant that they were dependent on the support of a number of men, like Slingsby, who did not fully share nor even understand the objectives that they were pursuing. Through experience and interest, the opposition leaders had acquired a skill and even a professional approach to politics that set them apart from the majority of MPs, who were for the most part country gentlemen and merchants chosen to represent the needs and interests of their town or locality in the traditionally limited and occasional functions of parliament. Nowhere in their experience, or in their concept of government by king-in-parliament, was there an independent role for parliament. Yet this was what the campaign to restrict and limit Charles in the free exercise of his powers was gradually creating. The further the opposition travelled in this direction, the more likely they were to shed much-needed supporters along the way.

The opposition campaign was mostly conducted with as much caution as the circumstances allowed, increasing only gradually the power of parliament to restrict and constrain the king. The impeachment of ministers such as Laud and Strafford was not new, and the *Triennial Act* of February 1641 gave parliament the right to sit each third year but did not preclude the king from calling and dissolving it as he wished within that framework. Moreover, it did nothing to change parliament's powers when it was in session. The execution of Strafford might make it more difficult for the king to find ministers to carry out his plans, but it only showed parliament's ability to call bad ministers to account in a similar way to the old device of impeachment.

In June 1641 a more significant step was taken with the presentation to the king of the *Ten Propositions*, which attempted to define rules and procedures for the future conduct of government, including a right of parliament to approve (or, by implication, reject) the king's choice of ministers and councillors. Important as this claim was, it was still expressed in suitably respectful terms. It was requested that the king should 'take into his Council for managing of the great affairs of this kingdom such officers and counsellors as his people and parliament may have just cause to confide in'. For the politically naïve, who might take such a request at face value, there was little that could be considered offensive in this. Only a consideration of how the arrangement might work in practice and of what might be the case if parliament did not have confidence in a chosen minister would bring out the vital implications of the king's agreement to such a proposition.

Through such careful drafting and presentation of their plans the opposition were able, for the most part, to carry the majority of MPs with them. But the further they progressed, the more difficult the task became. By the summer of 1641 there were ominous cracks appearing in the façade of unity. Some, like Gervase Holles and Lord George Digby, were disturbed by the means used to pursue Strafford, while others, like Edward Hyde, feared that the balance of power in government was being too greatly disturbed. Many of the back-benchers felt that their purposes had been achieved, and saw no reason to linger unnecessarily in the heat and squalor of London in summer when their own affairs required their attention. It is important not to exaggerate divisions at this stage, but there are signs that by the early summer of 1641 the opposition campaign was beginning to falter. This was just as they began to address that most contentious and divisive of all the issues facing them: the control and organisation of the Church.

ii) Religious Issues and Divisions

> **KEY ISSUES** In what ways did religious opinions among MPs vary? Why were religious issues difficult to deal with?

'We all agree' stated Lord George Digby in December 1640, '... that a Reformation of Church government is most necessary'. There is no doubt that religious grievances played a large part in bringing about the crisis of 1640, but it is equally clear that the nature and extent of these grievances varied. The Anglican Church rested on a compromise, and like all compromises it met with criticism from a variety of quarters. Since the reign of Elizabeth there had been those who considered that the Reformation had stopped short and who wished to carry on the task of purifying the Church of popish remnants and practices. They compared the discipline and liturgy (services and prayers) of England unfavourably with those practised in the Presbyterian system of Scotland. With the accession in England of James I in 1603 the comparisons became more acute, but with considerable skill the new king forged a compromise to suit his political needs and by cautious steps began to bring the Scottish system into line with the English use of bishops as the means of maintaining royal control. The issues that he faced and the methods that he used have been outlined earlier, in Chapter 1 – for clarification of some of the terms and ideas discussed below, refer back to the profile of religious issues on pp. 7–8.

The essential base for this compromise lay in the undoubted and unchallengeable acceptance by the king, and the vast majority of his bishops, of Calvinist doctrines. These were the Protestant beliefs laid down and practised by John Calvin in the Church that he had founded in Geneva. At their heart was the idea of predestination, a belief that salvation could not be earned or chosen by individuals (as Catholics and Arminians taught) but was a free gift from God, granted to those whom he had chosen and pre-destined to be saved and to live eternally among his 'saints'. These 'saints' were to be identified by their religious devotion and their constant struggle to live according to God's Will. This created Puritan concerns about rituals, ceremonies and the absence of Presbyterian discipline to help them in this struggle, but James's Puritan critics had no need to doubt the Protestant identity of the Church, and its total rejection of Rome and all its works. It was the destruction of this compromise by Charles and Archbishop Laud that gave rise to religious grievances in England, as well as provoking open rebellion in Scotland.

These grievances can be categorised at three broad levels. At the highest level were the small minority of Presbyterians who favoured a fully Calvinist system, with the Church purified and a discipline administered by ministers and lay elders as in Scotland. A much larger number of people (and MPs) desired a simplified form of worship and an emphasis on a preaching and teaching ministry, but had no objection to the use of bishops as a form of administration. Beyond this, the vast majority of the English feared and detested the name and idea of popery as a threat to their liberties, their souls, and their national survival.

The achievement of Charles and Laud had been to offend at all of these levels. Their interpretation of Arminian doctrines involved four key developments:

- increasing the authority of the Church and the clergy;
- welcoming all without making a distinction between 'saints' and sinners;
- promising salvation through the Church rather than through prayer and Bible-reading;
- utilising set prayers and ceremonies to create a sense of reverence described by Laud as 'the beauty of holiness'.

While this was attractive to some, it did represent, in both doctrine and organisation, a step closer to the ideas of the Catholic Church. Thus it threatened the established practices and doctrines of the Church and seemed, deliberately or otherwise, to open the way for the triumph of the imagined Catholic conspiracy that (in the eyes of contemporaries) threatened not only their religion but their political liberties as well. Hence the broad agreement to which Digby referred. The nation knew what it did not like and it did not like Laud and his works.

Nor were the majority of MPs prepared to accept the political role that the bishops had played. Laud's role as a Privy Councillor and the appointment of Bishop Juxon as Lord Treasurer from 1636 were greatly resented, as was the existence of a solid block of obedient votes in the House of Lords through the presence of the 26 bishops there. So strong was this resentment of episcopal interference in secular politics that in January 1641 Charles had agreed to dismiss them from government office, thus accepting a significant restriction on his freedom of choice. But he had insisted on retaining them in the Upper House. By 1 May, even before the execution of Strafford, the Commons had passed a bill to exclude them from the House of Lords, which was finally rejected by the Upper House in June [offering a good example of how the bishops' votes could influence political decisions]. Nevertheless the matter was pursued and in February 1642, when the Upper House was more under the control of the king's opponents, the Clerical Disabilities Act finally removed the bishops' temporal authority (in matters outside the Church) and seats in the Lords.

To this extent – but only to this extent – religious grievances united the nation in opposition to the king and his archbishop. To agree what they did not want was a simple matter; to agree on what should replace it was far more difficult. The alternative proposed in the *Root and Branch Bill,* which was introduced in the Commons at the end of May 1641, was a Presbyterian system similar to that which had been restored in Scotland. The terminology of 'Root and Branch' indicated the desire to abolish or 'root out' bishops completely, and destroy all the branches of officialdom that they had created. However, that did not necessarily mean that members wanted to replace them with a powerful Presbyterian clergy. While many MPs and their constituents accepted Calvinist doctrines and practices, they had no intention of handing over the discipline of the Church and the right of judgement over their morals and behaviour to churchmen of any kind. Indeed, part of their dislike of Laud stemmed from resentment at clerical pretensions, as illustrated by his use of Church courts and control of appointments. As Digby put it, to accept Presbyterian discipline would mean that 'instead of every bishop we put down in a Diocese, we shall set up a pope in every Parish'.

Other, perhaps more central, concerns can be seen in an extract from the diary of Sir Henry Slingsby.

Of God,   Of Man,   Of the Divell.

The Orthodox true Minister,   the Seducer and false Prophet.

Religious problems as seen from both sides of the political and
religious spectrum

1   I went with the Bill for taking away [the bishops'] votes in the House of
     Peers and to stop them from meddling with temporal affairs but I was
     against the Bill for taking away the function and calling of Bishops ... I
     could never be of the opinion that the government of the Church, as it
5   is now established by Bishops and Archbishops is an absolute necessity,
     so that taking them away would overturn the state and essence of a
     Christian church; but I am of the opinion that taking of them out of
     the Church ... may be of dangerous consequence to the peace of the
     Church ... Considering that this government hath continued from
10   the Apostles ... it were not safe to make alteration from so ancient a
     beginning.

For Slingsby the existence of episcopacy church government by bishops was not a matter of faith but of political and social discipline. The Church was an institution of state and a major form of social control in a society that lacked effective methods of law enforcement. The obedience of the people depended on acceptance of the social hierarchy and the teaching of deference – if that was destroyed in the Church, where would it be threatened next? It is significant that, when war came, both Digby and Slingsby would fight on the side of the king. Edward Hyde, who became the leader of a moderate royalist group in the Commons also cited the introduction of the Root and Branch Bill as crucial in his decision to break with the opposition party. Not for the last time, the adherents of Presbyterian discipline were to find their schemes rejected by a large number of their countrymen, many of whom shared their religious preferences in other ways. While some were merely reacting against clerical control of their lives and behaviour, others had far wider concerns regarding the role and place of the Church. While Slingsby disliked the bishops' claim to a power received directly from God, he found Laud's emphasis on ritual and ceremony preferable to the Puritan insistence on preaching, teaching and the importance of individual conscience, which he regarded as politically dangerous. Many MPs, and those who elected them, shared the widespread conservatism that regarded the Anglican Church, headed by the monarch and governed by bishops, as a guarantee of stability in society.

This reaction was considerably sharpened in 1641 by the emergence, in London at least, of a radical underworld, which confirmed their worst fears. The weakening of the bishops' control that had resulted from the attack on their powers had permitted small groups of Puritan separatists, who had previously met in secret, to operate far more openly. In addition, the breakdown of censorship had released a flood of pamphlets expressing radical ideas about religion and society. Nothing could illustrate more clearly to a conservative mind the dreadful consequences of removing the power and control of the Church over the people, and of the bishops over the Church. In that sense the rejection in June of Root and Branch reform, entailing the abolition of episcopacy, was part of a wider conservative reaction, which was beginning to take shape. To the extent that it gathered and focussed conservative unease about how far the opposition leaders were prepared to go in their struggle with the king, the religious issue was a major factor in the emergence, in the middle of 1641, of a king's party, which could significantly alter the likely outcome of the crisis.

iii) The Emergence of the Royalists

KEY ISSUE How and why did a royalist party develop in the House of Commons?

In November 1640, civil war was impossible because the king did not have a party large enough to fight for him. By the summer of 1641 this was changing, and by January 1642 when Charles attempted to arrest the Five Members he clearly believed that he was strong enough to take the initiative. Therefore, if we are to explain why war eventually broke out, we need to understand why, by 1642, many were ready to support him and why the king was sufficiently aware of this to bring matters to a head. It is not merely a matter of explaining why, once war was imminent, many were drawn back to old loyalties or found themselves unable to commit the sin of rebellion. If we are to understand why war became possible at all, we need to explain the emergence, by the autumn of 1641, of a sizeable group of people who were prepared to resist Pym's junto in parliament and to try to rally support for the king.

It is also important to emphasise that the men in question were not attempting to undo the achievements of 1640 and early 1641. Led by Edward Hyde and Lucius Carey, Lord Falkland, they sought a compromise that would restrain the king from further unconstitutional acts, guarantee the rule of law and the rights of parliament, and leave intact the valid powers of the king in both Church and state. Their concept of government was the harmonious partnership of king-in-parliament. Hence one reason for their emergence was the growing perception that by June 1641, with steps such as the Ten Propositions, the opposition was going too far in destroying the balance that they sought. In this sense the moderate royalists were true conservatives, seeking to preserve what they saw as the traditional balance between government, law, and individual or local rights and liberties. Thus they were further offended and confirmed in their dislike of Pym's junto by the Militia Bill and the Grand Remonstrance of late 1641 (see p. 48).

Conservatism was also a major influence on their religious outlook. Yet for many royalists there was more involved than a preference for traditional forms and a concern to maintain spiritual and intellectual control over the masses. Without accepting the high-flown claims of Laud that bishops inherited their authority in a direct line from the Apostles and thus from Christ himself, there were many who had come to value the Anglican faith for its own sake. The middle way adopted in the Elizabethan settlement had been successfully defended by Richard Hooker just before his death in 1600. In his *Laws of Ecclesiastical Polity* he had argued that Anglican practice truly reflected the spirit of early Christianity, shorn of the corrupting influence of popery, and that the functions of the bishops and the remaining ceremonies were to ensure good order and decency in worship. As such, they were therefore neither necessary for salvation, nor any barrier to it, and men could maintain their own opinions while accepting the need for the monarch, and his chosen advisers, to make decisions regarding their use in a national church.

These arguments struck a chord among men who were coming to the conclusion that religious differences should be minimised. The intellectual development of the early seventeenth century and a growing interest in the scientific study of the natural world was helping to generate distaste for both superstition and religious bigotry. It was no coincidence that both Hyde and Falkland had been members of an intellectual circle which met to discuss such issues at Falkland's home, Great Tew in Gloucestershire. There were men on both sides of the political divide of 1642 who shared this outlook, and in this sense Hyde and Falkland had much in common with Lord Brooke, who raised a regiment for parliament in 1642, and the Puritan intellectual, John Milton. In their case, a rational approach to religion led eventually to a belief in religious toleration. Hyde and others regarded such freedom for the masses as politically dangerous, and preferred the middle way adopted by the Elizabethan and Jacobean Church. While they rejected the clericalism of Laud, they had no intention of replacing it with the Presbyterian clericalism of the *Root and Branch Bill*. This emotion was most clearly expressed by Digby (see p. 39) but it was also a factor in the affection and loyalty felt by other royalists for the moderate, balanced, Anglican compromise that had been familiar to them before Laud. The survival of Anglican practice and use of the Prayer Book throughout the war and after is evidence of its popularity and enduring support at all levels of society.

Thus conservatism, based on a desire for what was believed to be the traditional balance in Church and state, seems to have been of crucial importance in the formation of a royalist group in parliament. However, Conrad Russell has pointed to another aspect, which combined and overlapped with these views – a resistance to Scottish interference and dictation. In *The Causes of the English Civil War* he argues that the Scots had 'an imperial vision' in which English practice in Church and state would be adapted to that of Scotland, and in which the imposition of Presbyterian practice in the Church was a key element [*Causes of the English Civil War*]. There is certainly no doubt that the Scottish Covenanters – the Presbyterians who had led the rebellion of 1637 and the subsequent invasion of England – did desire to spread Presbyterian practice to England. They made it the price of their support for the opposition in 1640–1, the condition of their alliance with parliament in 1643, and in their agreement with the king in December 1647. According to Russell, 'Those who emerged as anti-Scots in the first four months of the Long Parliament were Sir John Holland, Sir William Widdrington, Sir William Pennyman, Sir John Strangeways, Charles Price, Dr. Turner, John Selden, Edward Hyde, Sir Ralph Hopton, Arthur Capel and George Digby. Save for Selden and Sir John Holland, this list is almost a roll-call of the inner ring of the royalist party in the Commons and it merely confirms the point that the list of anti-Scots soon clearly included Falkland, Culpepper, Kirton and Waller. The Royalist party was an anti-Scottish party before it was a Royalist party'.

There were, therefore, a number of different but probably over-lapping reasons for the growth of a royalist group during the summer and autumn of 1641. Most significantly there was a dislike of the lengths to which Pym and his allies were taking the campaign and of the methods they were employing. There was fear for the balance of the constitution and of popular involvement in political activity. In addition, there was affection for the Anglican Church stripped of Laudian pretensions and dislike of clericalism of all kinds, particularly in its Scottish version. It is clear that the leaders of the group shared many of these perceptions, although which of them weighed most heavily with the uncommitted is more difficult to say. There is little doubt that, given real control over the king's actions, advisers such as Hyde could have won over large numbers and could probably have isolated the opposition. They were hindered, however, by the king's tendency, at crucial times, to listen to less balanced advice, for example a second scheme for an armed dissolution of parliament revealed by Pym in October. The result was that from June 1641 to January 1642 the battle for support was finely balanced and neither the royalist nor the opposition group could take decisive steps. Developments in this period created a situation of stalemate – but not yet the likelihood of war.

iv) The Junto and its Difficulties

KEY ISSUE Why did the opposition continue with their plans?

Members of the opposition were, therefore, able to maintain a considerable measure of support and sympathy, but faced an increasingly desperate struggle to preserve the parliamentary unity that they required if they were to guarantee the safety of their reforms and of themselves. In these circumstances, it is necessary to ask why the opposition leadership persisted with reforms and measures in two areas where their support was clearly weak – the abolition of bishops in favour of a Presbyterian system, and the further restriction of the king's power. The latter can be explained fairly simply, for it was impossible to stop the process that had begun until there was some guarantee of the permanence of what had been achieved. Unless they could trust Charles, or limit his powers so tightly that he could not undo their work (or threaten their lives and estates), the members of the opposition were bound to continue with what they had started. The religious issue was more complex, involving a number of possible motives, some based on deeply held convictions, others upon personal or political necessity.

In the first place, for many of the opposition leaders religious reform was not a matter of politics but of principle. For men such as Oliver St. John and Nathaniel Fiennes the abolition of episcopacy was an issue of conscience. Some of them believed in the necessity of Presbyterian discipline, but for others the strongest argument was the corrupting influence of bishops who obstructed preaching and encouraged idolatry. For those who believed that the way to God was through private prayer, the study of the Bible, and the teaching of God's word, the rituals and organisation imposed by the bishops were a positive barrier to individual salvation and conspired to maintain ignorance and darkness in society. They believed that only when this barrier was removed would true religion flourish and the 'reformation of manners' in society begin. By no means all of the opposition shared this view. Some political tacticians favoured Root and Branch reform because it would serve to weaken the king's control of the Church, and therefore his ability to make changes in the future. There was also another, more compelling reason for presenting the scheme to parliament – as indicated above, it was the price demanded by the Scottish Covenanters for their continued support, and without them the opposition would be lost. It should not be forgotten that the continued existence of the Long Parliament derived from the king's need for money to maintain his agreement with the Scots. If their support should be withdrawn, then the hopes of the opposition, and probably their lives and fortunes would be lost with it.

Thus, for a variety of reasons and motives, the opposition was committed to the abolition of episcopacy and would be unable to give way on this matter even if it cost them the chance of a settlement or vital parliamentary support. It is impossible to be sure which of these concerns weighed most heavily. John Morrill has emphasised the importance of religion as a motive within the parliamentarian group, and has argued that it is underestimated in Russell's attribution of such great influence to the Scots. This view is explained in an essay entitled 'England's Wars of Religion' in his essay collection *The Nature of the English Revolution*. There is no doubt that, again and again in the events of the Civil War period, religious zeal distinguished those who were willing to push on to adopt ever more extreme or dangerous measures from those who sought to compromise or to put a brake on the process of change. What Morrill calls 'Puritan dynamism' was a real and important element in parliamentarian thinking. In terms of the *Root and Branch Bill* and the influence of the Scots, it is impossible to be sure, except in individual cases, which motive was paramount. It should also be pointed out that the Scottish Covenanters were themselves motivated by Puritan convictions and a missionary zeal to spread the true faith. Whatever the precise mixture of motives behind its presentation, the rejection of the *Root and Branch Bill* by the House of Commons in June 1641 was a severe blow to Pym and his associates, and marked the opening of a religious division which, more clearly than any other single issue, defined the opposing parties or 'sides' into which the nation would fall within a year.

By the summer of 1641, therefore, there were signs of a weakening in the opposition leaders' position and an improvement in that of the king. Encouraged by this to see a possible way out of his difficulties, Charles announced in June that he would visit Scotland in August, in order to ratify the Treaty of Ripon. His real intentions are unclear, but there were signs of the emergence of a royalist party in Edinburgh and his choice of the royalist Earl of Morton as his Chancellor in August 1641 suggests that he may have been trying to build up their strength. If so, he acted with a lack of political tact, promising co-operation with the Scottish parliament on the one hand and selecting officers who were offensive to it on the other. The result was that he failed to establish the support that he required but demonstrated once more to the opposition and the uncommitted in both kingdoms that he was considering conflicting strategies. For the opposition leaders in London this was a time of great difficulty and danger. Their fears of Charles's activities in Scotland were widely shared among their sympathisers. According to Lucy Hutchinson, the wife of the staunchly Puritan Colonel John Hutchinson,

1   The king's design in going to Scotland was variously conjectured; but
    this was a certain effect of it, that it retarded all the affairs of the gov-
    ernment of England, which the king had put into such disorder that it
    was not an easy task to reform what was amiss and redress the real
5   grievances of the people.

In late August came the parliamentary recess, a time when the opposition leaders were at their most vulnerable to attack or arrest, and it was not unreasonable that they feared for their lives and liberties if the king should succeed in freeing himself of his problems with the Scots. If he could freely use the military strength at his disposal then they might well find themselves seized as rebels and traitors, the parliament dismissed, and the reforms that they had achieved thus far reversed and destroyed. That this did not occur can be attributed to two factors. The first was Charles's lack of judgement and political skill in dealing with the Scots. The second arose from his kingdom across the water – the outbreak of rebellion in Ireland at the end of October 1641.

e) The Second Turning-point: The Irish Rebellion

> **KEY ISSUES** How did the Irish rebellion affect the relationships between the king and different MPs? Why did it trigger the outbreak of civil war?

In the early autumn of 1641 an Irish population which had seen much of its land pass into the hands of English and Scottish settlers and had suffered the heavy hand of Lord Deputy Strafford, seized the opportunity offered by his demise and the king's preoccupation with other matters, to rise in armed revolt. It is difficult to exaggerate either the impact or the significance of the Irish rebellion in the sequence of events which led from the crisis of 1640–1 to the war of 1642. For the English Protestant, the Irish combined the menace of an uncivilised race with the demonology of popery. As the stories of Catholic atrocities against their Protestant neighbours filtered across the water during October and November, the fear and tension rose and with it the need for action to suppress the rebels. Yet, to the fury of MPs, the king chose to linger in Scotland, not returning until 17 November to an England rife with rumours of Irish invasion. In Yorkshire, for example, church services were interrupted with the news that the Irish had landed in Lancashire that day, had already reached Rochdale and would shortly be in Bradford. Logically, such speed of movement was impossible, but the ˚panicking congregation in Bradford were apparently prepared to believe anything of those who did the devil's work! To some extent this reflects the deep-seated and irrational fear of popery that existed in seventeenth-century England, but fear of Catholic invasion did have some foundation in reality. It was not that the Irish rebels themselves constituted a threat to England and its government, but that Ireland as a base for attack by Catholic powers such as France and Spain was a real possibility, particularly if they should be invited by a king who was under threat from his parliament, a king with a French Catholic wife.

In these circumstances Charles lost both credibility and his chances of ridding himself of a troublesome parliament. According to Richard Baxter,

1   there was nothing that with the people wrought so much [had so much effect] as the Irish massacre and rebellion ... This filled all England with a fear both of the Irish and of the Papists at home ... And when they saw the English Papists join with the king against the parliament it was
5   the greatest thing that ever alienated them from the king.

An army had to be raised to suppress the rebels and an army must be paid for – and only parliamentary subsidies could provide the necessary finance. Accordingly Charles asked the Commons for help in raising forces and thereby presented the opposition with an impossible dilemma. To refuse resources for an army needed to rescue Protestant settlers was unthinkable – as unthinkable as placing them at the disposal of a king whom they did not trust, whom they suspected was a secret Catholic or at least a Catholic sympathiser, and who had made it perfectly clear on more than one occasion that he considered a violent or military solution to his problems to be both attractive and justified. Nor was this a dilemma that could be left or put aside. Action was needed in Ireland and delay could be fatal.

Thus, in the months that followed, both king and opposition were being forced by the Irish rebellion to act in haste and both therefore took up more extreme positions than they otherwise might have done. On 8 November Pym succeeded in attaching the condition that the king should employ only 'such councillors as should be approved by parliament' to the offer of forces, and on 7 December Sir Arthur Haselrig moved that the army raised should be placed under the control of a general appointed by parliament. This proposal, known as the *Militia Bill*, the term Militia meaning an army, involved a major encroachment on the king's established powers and prerogative which would not only be unacceptable to the king himself but also greatly offended many in the House of Commons. For those such as Edward Hyde, who sought a settlement that would secure the rights and liberties of the subject within the existing structure, such radical measures would destroy the balance of the constitution and change the nature of government. They were therefore even more infuriated by the second part of Pym's tactics. Under the guise of a petition to the king he introduced the *Grand Remonstrance*, a statement of the grievances of the nation, which recalled the abuses of the 1630s, reminded the MPs of what they had achieved by their unity thus far, and laid out the reforms that were still required. As a justification of the opposition campaign to rally parliament to their cause, it was skilful and effective. That it was passed in the Commons by the narrow margin of eleven votes is evidence of the difficulties faced by the opposition leaders at this stage. What ultimately outraged the king and his sympathisers was that on 15 December the decision was taken to publish the *Remonstrance* in an open appeal to the nation at large. In the eyes of cautious men this was not only an unprecedented insult to the king, it was also a dangerous incitement of popular opinion and an invitation to the people to involve themselves in what was rightly the business of the governing classes.

Charles's response to these provocations helped to polarise the political nation further. In December he rejected the *Remonstrance* out of hand. Evidence of popular displeasure at this was provided in the elections for the Mayor and Common Council of the City of London on 22 December, which produced a large majority of opposition support. Charles tried to counter this, and in fact increased it, by appointing the brutal Sir Thomas Lunsford as Lieutenant of the Tower of London in an attempt to overawe the city. By the end of December it was clear that events were slipping beyond the control of either party. There was growing support in parliament and country for the king, as gentlemen of moderate and traditional outlook grew increasingly disturbed by the radicalism of the opposition. In late December the bishops were temporarily prevented from sitting in the House of Lords by popular demonstrations. When they demanded on their return that all proceedings in their absence be declared null and void, the lay Lords rejected this as an infringement of their privileges. The arrogance of the bishops infuriated many of them, and this was a matter of concern for the king. Convinced that his support was growing, and determined to act quickly to forestall any alliance of Lords and Commons over this matter, Charles attempted to seize the initiative. On 3 January he requested the Lords that they send one of their members, Lord Kimbolton, and five MPs for trial. Having received no response, on 4 January 1642 he entered the House of Commons (in itself a breach of their privileges) to arrest the five MPs – Pym, Haselrig, Hampden, Holles and Strode. Finding that they had been warned and escaped to safety in the city, the king declared that he intended nothing more than legal measures against them, an assurance rendered less than convincing by the fact that he was accompanied to the House by an escort of 400 armed men.

The attempt, and its failure, was a serious mistake. Suspicions that he was willing to use force to override opposition were confirmed, his apparent lack of respect for his subjects' rights and liberties was reinforced, and many waverers were convinced that the measures taken by the opposition were necessary. Popular demonstrations in London increased, and were probably only partly orchestrated by Pym and his allies. Isolated, and possibly afraid of mob violence against his family, the king left London on 10 January. According to John Morrill in the volume of essays cited above, this was probably another serious misjudgement. The opposition control of the Commons was by no means secure, and if Charles had remained in London to rally his sympathisers they might yet have swung the House in his favour. As it was, they had to demonstrate their loyalty by leaving it. Morrill argues that 'One of the striking things about parliamentary divisions in the months after the Attempt on the Five Members and ... the royal retreat from London is the way Pym's majority remained constant in a rapidly dwindling House. If half of those who had voted against the Grand Remonstrance, and who subsequently abandoned London with the king, had stayed put, it is unlikely that any of the major escalations towards war could have been put through the House of Commons'. As it was, Pym had a free hand. Utilising the king's isolation and unpopularity, he pushed through the *Clerical Disabilities Act*, which excluded the bishops from the House of Lords, and transformed the uncompleted *Militia Bill* into an Ordinance, which did not require the king's assent. It was approved by a depleted House of Lords in February 1642.

Thereafter, it is difficult to envisage any peaceful outcome of the struggle, although it was not until August that the king formally embarked on war by raising his standard at Nottingham. The descent into civil war was slow, piecemeal, and often reluctant, quite in accordance with Whitelocke's bemused claim that it was unsought and unplanned (see p.21). The spring and early summer saw a jockeying for political and military advantage, as both sides tried to secure their position, but many of the military preparations were essentially defensive in character, as if both parties were reluctant to take any initiative that might remove lingering hopes of settlement. There is little doubt that the king's removal from London to York increased the opposition's fear of attack. It is significant that it was in January 1642 that they took steps to ensure that the great royal arsenal kept in Hull was under the control of a governor nominated by parliament, Sir John Hotham. In April the king attempted to gain control of Hull, and was denied entry by Sir John. It is interesting, in the light of Hotham's later attempt to change sides, that he refused to give up the arms without a warrant from both king and parliament. In a confused and difficult situation Hotham's actions may well have represented, not so much committed support for parliament, as a refusal to take sides at all. He simply stuck rigidly to what he perceived as his duty. By declaring him a traitor for his actions and refusing to withdraw this when parliament took responsibility in Hotham's defence, Charles ultimately made Hotham's decision for him.

A propaganda battle followed in which both sides sought to justify their actions in the light of aggression by the other. Parliament sent out orders for the raising of the militia, locally based volunteer forces, and the king issued similar orders, commissions of array, in June – the unfortunate magistrates who received these orders were thereby forced to decide which, if either, to obey. A series of skirmishes took place in different counties as the committed supporters of both parties tried to secure the area and its administration for their use. In a final attempt at settlement, parliament presented the king with the *Nineteen Propositions* (see Appendix) but since these included parliamentary control of the militia, restrictions on the king's choice of advisers and reform of the Church by a national synod (assembly of ministers), they can hardly have expected that he would find them acceptable. It is more likely that the propositions represented the minimum safeguards that the opposition leaders felt they required. Charles's reply was a masterly statement of the royalist case, in which he firmly claimed the moral and legal high ground; arguing that England already had a balanced constitution and that the powers of parliament were sufficient to prevent 'the evil of absolute monarchy ... which is tyranny' he claimed that further change would spark off a worse evil, an uprising of the common people.

Conrad Russell has raised questions about the reasons why there was so little serious negotiation in the spring and summer of 1642, suggesting that the possibility of a Scottish alliance distracted both sides from the recognition that they had to find some solution for their difficulties

Causes of the Civil War, p. 222. While this is a possibility, it seems more likely that the crucial factor was the endemic lack of trust between the parties. It is impossible to believe that, by this stage, either side could have faith in the promises of the other, and the propaganda battle of the spring had undoubtedly deepened mutual suspicions. John Morrill in *The Nature of the English Revolution* has also drawn attention to the growing anarchy in the provinces, created by a weakness if not a breakdown of normal administration coupled with an increasing intensity of popular feeling. This, he points out, has been thoroughly documented by Anthony Fletcher in his *Outbreak of the Civil War*. Morrill argues that concern about a growing level of popular demonstrations was a major influence in driving conservative gentlemen into the king's party, and in forcing the parliament to take action to maintain control. Some of the unrest was stirred up by parties themselves, but there is also evidence, for example in enclosure riots and in the destruction of recent drainage works by dispossessed fen-dwellers in East Anglia, that the lower classes were taking advantage of the situation for their own ends. What is clear from this confused picture is that the war was indeed unplanned; the most logical explanation of the actions of both parties in the early months of 1642 is that in both cases they believed that they were the victims of the other's actual or intended aggression, and in both cases, they ultimately took up arms in their own defence.

3 Conclusion; From Crisis to Conflict

> **KEY ISSUE** Why did the crisis end in war rather than in a settlement?

In 1640 the monarchy and the system of government in England was in crisis because the governing class on whom the king relied was offended by the actions and practices that he had adopted since his accession in 1625. Faced with long-term difficulties in finance, in the need to govern three different kingdoms (each with its own culture and traditions) and, above all, by religious divisions which cut across these national boundaries, Charles's attempts to find solutions which accorded with his own political and religious convictions had succeeded only in alienating the majority of his subjects. With hindsight it is possible to see that a genuine compromise was always unlikely, because the king did not believe it to be necessary. His belief in the divine authority that he held, and in the forms of government that he was establishing in Church and state, was unshakeable, and although he could be forced into concessions (as he was in 1640 and 1641) it was always clear that he regarded these as temporary and felt no obligation to maintain them any longer than he was forced to. When he did listen to the advice of his more moderate and astute councillors, for example in calling parliament in

1628 and again in 1640, he found it impossible to establish a compromise which did not offend his own deepest convictions.

As a result, the attempt by the opposition in parliament to use their financial power to bring him to a settlement was doomed to failure, because without his sincere commitment to uphold any agreement, there was no point at which they could feel secure in the gains that had been made. Essentially, the king saw them as rebels and, if restored to the free exercise of his powers, would be likely to treat them as such. To that extent the possibility of a military outcome to the crisis had always existed. The king was willing to use force to solve his problems because, in his view, he had the right to do so. What he lacked in 1640–1 was the means. Thus, the first steps toward civil war were taken in the summer and autumn of 1641 when the emergence of a royalist party within parliament made it possible for the king to fight. In that sense, the doubtful legality of Strafford's execution, the constitutional issues raised by further attempts to limit the king's power, and particularly the religious issues raised by the desire to reform the Church, were all causes of the war, since they contributed greatly to the development of a royalist party.

This revival in the king's fortunes created fear and tension in the ranks of the opposition, but it did not necessarily lead to civil war. The reluctance with which military measures were put into effect in 1642 indicates that both sides would have continued to seek political victory if given the time to engineer it. The leaders of the royalist party, such as Edward Hyde, were pursuing a compromise settlement, not the reversal of all that had been done since November 1640. What deprived the participants of the time to achieve any of these goals was the outbreak of rebellion in Ireland. Not only did it drive fear and tension to new heights by raising the threat of popery, it also created a problem that demanded an immediate, military solution. By bringing the power struggle into the open, it polarised the parties and by introducing a note of urgency it made a rapid resolution of the issues necessary. As a result, both sides took extreme actions – the publication of the *Grand Remonstrance* was an appeal to the people against the king, the attempt to arrest the Five Members an attack on the privileges of parliament and the lives and liberties of its members. Moreover, by raising a military problem, the rebellion increased the likelihood of a military solution. Once forces began to be raised the question of whom they would be used against was raised with them. In the end, men took up arms because they feared that, if they did not, they would be the victims of armed attack by others. 'I am not for a tame resignation of our religion, lives and liberties into the hands of our adversaries who seek to devour it', declared Whitelocke in 1642; and in the end it seemed, to both sides, that the only course of action open to them was to fight.

Working on Chapter 2

Making notes on 'From Crisis to Conflict'

(N.B. for general advice on effective note-making, see the Preface).

Explaining why the crisis of 1640 became the war of 1642 involves the examination of a series of actions and errors on the part of king and parliament, and of a sequence of events which led them to war. In other words, in order to understand why war occurred we have to establish how it came about. You will therefore need to make detailed notes which trace this sequence from November 1640 to August 1642. At the same time, the chapter also seeks to analyse certain issues in greater depth, and it may simplify your task if you make notes on these aspects of the period separately. It is therefore suggested that you:

1. Read through the entire chapter first.
2. Re-read and make notes based on the sub-headings provided in the chapter. The bulk of these notes using a sequential outline of events, in which you can signify key developments in two areas – the growth of mutual fear and distrust, and the gradual loss of unity in parliament. These notes will be drawn from sections 2a, 2c, 3a, 3d, 3e and 4.
3. In addition, you should make separate notes on certain key issues which are analysed in greater depth; (a) the nature of the opposition (section 2b); (b) religious issues (3b); (c) the nature of royalism (3c).

You will be able to make these notes as you work through the chapter, but it will be useful for you to use separate sheets of paper so that you can extract or slot them in as separate units.

Answering essay questions on Chapter 2

Most examination questions about this period focus on the central question of why civil war occurred in 1642. They may be phrased or presented in different ways, but they are essentially concerned with the same issue. It is therefore possible to prepare for a range of essay questions by defining certain themes or factors as central to the issue of why war broke out. One way of doing this is to begin with a time-line as you did after Chapter 1, but on this occasion, select events that helped to cause war. You should choose a long time span, per-haps from 1603–1642, so that you can show how problems built up. This allows you to establish some of the events that caused the crisis of 1640 [see Chapter 1] as well as the events in 1640–2. Arrange these events into factors, use different colours to show which events were linked to religion, financial problems, ruling different king-doms, the role of parliaments, and the personality of Charles.

You can therefore plan and write an essay response to the question, 'Why did civil war break out in England in 1642?' by using the five fac-tors of religious fears and divisions, financial problems for the crown,

Summary Diagram

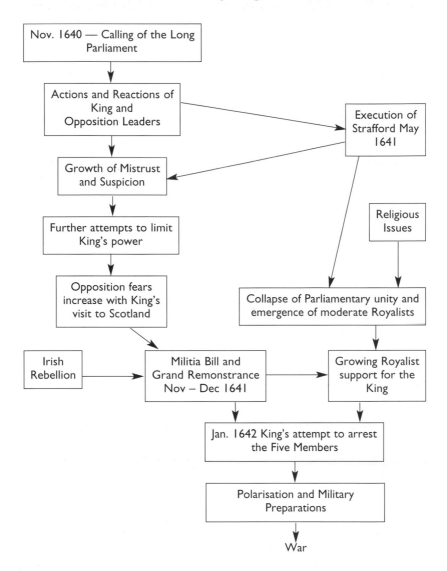

the difficulty of ruling three kingdoms, the growing independence of parliaments, and the personality/beliefs of Charles I. The best approach would probably be to arrange your material in three sections, explaining first what factors led to discontent and the crisis that came to a head with the calling of the Long Parliament in 1640, secondly how they interacted to increase mistrust and create two 'sides' by late 1641, and finally how the Irish Rebellion brought all the factors together to trigger a descent into war.

At AS level you are likely to be asked the question in this straight-forward way, either as a structured essay, e.g.

1a) Describe the problems that led to a crisis between king and parliament in November 1640.

1b) Why did the crisis lead to a war in 1642?

Or as a single question, e.g.

1. Account for the outbreak of civil war in England in 1642

At A2 level you may well be asked to make a judgement about the role of different factors, and consider their importance, e.g.

2. How far was Charles I responsible for the outbreak of war in 1642?

Question 1 can be approached as suggested above, but those like question 2 require you to adapt your material. If you begin with Charles I as a factor and explain his role and contribution to the war, then show that the other listed factors also played a part, you will be answering the question clearly. You can then analyse your explanation by summarising the role of each factor and coming to a judgement about theit relative importance.

Source exercise on Chapter 2

Re-read the five Sources from Chapter 2 pp. 21, 25, 41, 46, 47 and answer the following questions.

1. According to Baxter [p. 21], what grievances were expressed by MPs when the Long Parliament met in November 1640? [comprehension /inference] (*3 marks*)

2. a) What does Clarendon [p. 25] suggest about the different attitudes of Pym and Hyde in the early weeks of the Long Parliament? [inference/interpretation] (*4 marks*)

  b) How far can you rely on Hyde's evidence in this source? [evaluation] (*4 marks*)

3. a) What does the source on p. 41 reveal about the attitude of Slingsby towards the Church and the different proposals for religious reforms? [comprehension/inference] (*3 marks*)

  b) Using your own knowledge and the information in the source, explain why Slingsby fought for the king rather than parliament in 1642 and after. [interpretation in context, and synthesis] (*6 marks*)

4. What do Lucy Hutchinson and Baxter [pp. 46 and 47] reveal about the reasons for the mistrust of Charles that had developed by the end of 1641? [inference, analysis, cross-referencing] (*6 marks*)

5. Using the evidence from the sources as a whole, and your own knowledge, explain how far you would agree with the claim that it was religious fears and disputes that formed the main reason for the outbreak of civil war in England in 1642.

3 A Nation Divided, 1642–3

POINTS TO CONSIDER

The process by which England slipped into war in 1642 was not neat and decisive, but slow, reluctant and piecemeal. From the moment that Charles left London in January 1642, war was a possibility, but it was not until the failure of the peace negotiations at Oxford in May 1643 that it became an all-out struggle for victory. The intervening year is difficult to describe coherently, because events in many areas were not coherent. The list of key dates set out below illustrates the dual process of preparation for war and an increasingly desperate struggle to maintain peace. The main purpose of this chapter, therefore, is to analyse the patterns of division and allegiance that emerged, and to explain how and why they took this form. Hence it offers an opportunity to demonstrate how historians investigate complex issues by an in-depth analysis of sources, of the kind that you may be asked to carry out towards the end of your A-level course.

KEY DATES IN WAR AND PEACE

1642		
	January	Charles left London and set up his Court in York.
	February	Henrietta Maria sailed for Holland to raise money and forces.
	March	Parliament passed the Militia Bill as an Ordinance, not requiring royal assent.
	April	Charles was refused entry to the arms store at Hull.
	April–June	King and Parliament pursued a propaganda struggle over the incident at Hull.
	June	Parliament issued orders for the Militia. Charles issued Commissions of Array. Parliament presented the king with *Nineteen Propositions*, which the king rejected claiming that they would make him, 'but the shadow of a king'.
	July	The Navy declared for Parliament. Both parties appointed military commanders.
	August	The king raised his standard at Nottingham and called for volunteers. In Yorkshire a county meeting of freeholders agreed on a neutrality pact.
	September	Parliament began to organise county associations to control their forces. Staffordshire county freeholders declared their county a neutral zone.

	October	Battle of Edgehill
		Parliamentary forces in Yorkshire ended their
		neutrality agreement.
	November	Royalist army held at Turnham Green and
		prevented from seizing London.
		The king retreated to winter at Oxford.
	December	The Earl of Newcastle's army entered Yorkshire,
		and fortified York. JPs in Cheshire agreed the
		Treaty of Bunbury, banning armies from entering
		the county.
1643	**February**	Henrietta Maria arrived in York with arms from
		Holland. A 'Peace Party' in Parliament proposed
		negotiations with the king. They began in April.
	May	Failure of negotiations marked a new phase of
		intensive campaigning and all-out war.

KEY ISSUE How did the division of the country take shape?

---

1 The Process of Division

Although the official outbreak of the Civil War dates from August 1642, when the king raised his standard at Nottingham and called for volunteers, the process of division and the search for strategic advantage had begun some months before that, and continued for many months thereafter. In January 1642 the king left London. In February Henrietta Maria sailed for Holland to raise men and money for the king. In April the king was denied access to the arms in Hull by the parliamentarian governor, Sir John Hotham, and while the ensuing propaganda war raged between king and parliament, the weapons were hastily transferred to London. In June, while the *Nineteen Propositions* were theoretically still under discussion, both sides sent out orders to their county commissioners for the raising of troops. In July the navy declared for parliament and the Earl of Warwick was appointed Admiral, the king appointed the Marquess of Hertford as Lieutenant-General of his western armies, and the Earl of Essex was chosen for overall command of the parliamentary forces. In this context, the call for volunteers to Nottingham was only one more step, and not the final one, in the military division of the country.

It is difficult to piece together a coherent account of the early months of the war, since it consisted for the most part of military skirmishes designed to secure local or regional control. In August and September 1642 both sides were engaged in assembling volunteers and in securing strong points. Portsmouth, for example, was declared to be for the king by its governor, George Goring, in August but was captured for parliament by Sir William Waller in early September. A similar struggle was waged for Sherborne Castle. Here the Marquess of Hertford was besieged by parliamentarians until Sir Ralph Hopton was driven to join him after being defeated near Yeovil. With this extra strength, the royalists were able to hold the castle until they chose to evacuate it, Hertford leaving to organise recruits in South Wales and Hopton to secure Cornwall for the king. By December the struggle had resolved itself into four main theatres in which the protagonists were occupied for the winter and early spring. In the east and south-east the strength of parliamentarian feeling and the proximity of London allowed parliament's supporters to secure control, and to organise associations of counties (such as the Eastern Association) for military and administrative purposes. In the west, the midlands and the north, the outcome was more finely balanced.

However, in all areas, the conduct of the war was characterised by a marked reluctance by many to participate. Between June and October many county communities concluded local agreements to cease recruiting and prevent bloodshed within their own counties. Some went further, and, as in the Treaty of Bunbury drawn up in Cheshire in December 1642, agreed to raise a local force to prevent others fighting within their county boundaries. Some truces seem to have been part of a local conflict in which both sides sought a breathing-space, as in Devon in February 1643, but others represented genuine efforts to end or prevent war. From all parts of the country, accommodation petitions were sent to both king and parliament, begging them to resolve their differences by peaceful agreement. Throughout the winter and spring of 1642–3, until after the failure of the Oxford negotiations in May 1643, hopes of peace or a short-lived war survived to delay and complicate the process of division and the nature of military manoeuvres.

Already, however, parliament had come close to disaster, when the king attempted to resolve the whole issue by capturing London itself. In August he was joined at Nottingham by his nephews, Prince Rupert and Prince Maurice, who were experienced soldiers from the United Provinces (Holland). Thereafter he moved west to Shrewsbury to join up with his Welsh supporters and began a march towards the capital. Intercepted by parliament's main forces under the Earl of Essex, who had been based at Worcester, he fought an indecisive battle at Edgehill. Although the royalist cavalry succeeded in routing their opponents, their inability to regroup and rejoin the battle allowed the parliamentarian foot to retreat in good order. While the battle itself produced no clear-cut result, Essex's withdrawal to Warwick at the end of the day left the king's road to London clear, and Banbury and Oxford were both occupied by the royalists while Rupert stormed the town of Brentford. Only when Essex joined up with the London Trained Bands under Major-General Philip Skippon at Turnham Green on 13 November were the royalist forces held, and forced to retreat into winter quarters at Oxford. The campaign had shown the extent of early advantage held by the king. Unlike the parliament, he had a clear target to aim at (London) and hence a clear strategy. Able to draw on experienced cavalry among his supporters, he had defeated parliament's untried forces, and had Rupert's cavalry been as strong in discipline and tactics as as they were in attack, Edgehill might have been an outright and decisive victory for the king. Although not apparent at the time, the Edgehill campaign and a quick victory was probably the king's best chance of a successful outcome to the war.

Without such a rapid resolution of the conflict, the war now settled into a series of regional campaigns as both sides sought to secure their territorial base. This was necessary for both strategic advantage, and for supplies of men and money. In the north, the Earl of Newcastle was appointed commander of the king's forces and entered Yorkshire in early December to confront the local forces raised by the Fairfaxes. Although Fairfax was successful in the West Riding, York was held for the king, and in February 1643 the queen arrived there with arms brought from Holland via Bridlington. In June 1643 Newcastle inflicted a heavy defeat on the Fairfaxes at Adwalton Moor, forcing them to retreat into Hull which was the only stronghold in Yorkshire left in parliamentarian hands. Meanwhile, the struggle in the west had been finely balanced, with Hopton and the royalists secure in the south-west and Waller's parliamentarian forces achieving significant successes in South Wales, Somerset and Gloucestershire. In July 1643 a parliamentarian victory at Lansdown near Bath was negated by the defeat of Waller at Roundway Down near Devizes. In the same month, Prince Rupert successfully stormed the parliamentarian stronghold of Bristol, giving the royalist cause the advantage in the west. However, the success of the parliamentarian cavalry led by Oliver Cromwell in the eastern counties allowed parliament's forces to relieve Gainsborough in the east and extend their effective control north into Lincolnshire.

The late spring of 1643, therefore, produced no military outcome to the war, although the advantage lay with the royalists at that point. What was more important at this stage was that the struggle was clearly going to be prolonged, and any hopes of peace or neutrality entertained by those who were torn between, or uncommitted to, the warring parties were clearly shown to be illusory. To confirm this, the failure of negotiations that took place in Oxford during April and May 1643 showed how far apart the objectives of the two sides remained. In the words of Derek Hirst in his study of *Authority and Conflict, 1603–58.*

1   The spring of 1643, so agonising for those at Westminster and their supporters, was a watershed for the country. Despite the fulminations complaints of king and parliament, neutralism had until now been a perfectly logical response to the war. Did not both sides protest their
5   devotion to the same ideals in church and state? But the failure of new negotiations at Oxford that spring ... showed that whatever their rhetoric the two sides were far apart. There was now no escaping the conclusion that civil war had to be fought out. Thus it can be claimed that

the spring of 1643 was the end of the beginning. Then, and only then,
10 did it become valid to speak of a divided nation, and to consider and
examine the causes and nature of that division.

2 The Nature of Division

> **KEY ISSUES** What do contemporary sources reveal about the
> taking of sides? What factors influenced the patterns of
> allegiance that emerged?

a) Beliefs and Motivation

In the autumn of 1642 the country faced the stark reality of civil war
and slowly began to take sides. The nature of division and the patterns
of allegiance that emerged are described by contemporary observers
from both sides with a surprising degree of unanimity. According to
Clarendon,

1 Training as volunteers for parliament began to be practised in many
 places of the kingdom; but only in those corporations [towns] and by
 those inferior people who were notorious for faction and schism in
 religion
5 *[Schism means division, and Clarendon is probably referring to those who
 refused to accept the Anglican Church as it was – the puritans. He may also
 have had in mind those who had gone a step further, and left the Church to
 worship in private meetings – puritan separatists, although they were relatively few in number at this stage].*
10 The people generally (except in great towns and corporations
 where... the factious lecturers [preachers] and emissaries from parliament had poisoned the affections) and especially those of quality, were
 loyally inclined ... [In the West] most of the gentry were engaged
 against [the parliament] as they were in truth throughout the kingdom;
15 yet the common people, especially in the clothing parts of
 Somersetshire, were generally too much inclined to them ... [In
 Somerset the parliamentarian leaders were] for the most part clothiers
 ... though the gentlemen of ancient families and estates in that country
 were, for the most part, well-affected to the king ... [In Gloucestershire
20 it was] the yeomanry who had been most active and seditious, being
 very wealthy ... In Lancashire men of no name ... [and] the town of
 Manchester (out of factious humour and pride of their wealth) opposed
 the king. [In Yorkshire] besides the Lord Fairfax, there were in truth
 few of good reputation and fortune who ran that way ... Leeds, Halifax
25 and Bradford (three very populous and rich towns which, depending
 wholly upon clothiers, naturally maligned the gentry) were wholly at
 their disposition ...

Clarendon's analysis reveals something of the geographical division of the kingdom, for he deals mainly with the northern and western areas that came under royalist control, but emphasises much more strongly the class divisions which characterised the two sides. It is necessary to allow for some exaggeration in this matter, for to the seventeenth-century mind the loyalty and support of the gentry, the governing and social elite, would be of greatest value, and help to vindicate the cause for which they fought. Quite literally, these supporters represented the best of society. In this case, however, Clarendon's account is borne out by those of parliamentarian supporters such as Richard Baxter and Thomas May. According to Baxter,

1   A great part of the Lords forsook the parliament, and so did many of the House of Commons, and came to the king; but that was after Edgehill fight [October 1642] when the king was at Oxford. A very great part of the knights and gentlemen ... adhered to the king; except in Middlesex,
5   Essex, Suffolk, Norfolk, Cambridgeshire etc., where the king with his army never came. And if he could have got footing there, it is likely that it would have been there as it was in other places. And most of the tenants of these gentlemen and also most of the poorest of the people, whom the other called 'the rabble' did follow the gentry and were for
10 the king. On the parliament's side were (besides themselves) some of the gentry in most counties, and the greatest part of the tradesmen and freeholders, and the middle sort of men, especially in those corporations and countries which depend on clothing and such manufactures.

There seems little doubt, therefore, that parliament drew much support from the middle ranks of society, particularly in the urban and manufacturing areas. Examples of volunteers from these socio-economic groups can be found all over the country, but particularly in the clothing areas of West Yorkshire, Somerset and Gloucestershire. The urban support for the cause is evidenced by the role played by key urban centres in holding up the royalist advance on London in 1643. Bristol was captured after a short siege, but Plymouth, Gloucester and Hull withstood the royalist attacks. Nor, in Baxter's eyes, was there any uncertainty about the reason for this.

1   If you ask the reasons of this [he continued] ask also why in France it is not commonly the nobility nor the beggars, but the merchants and middle sort of men that [are] Protestants. The reasons which the parliament's supporters themselves gave was because (say they) the
5   tradesmen have a correspondency with London, and so are grown to be a far more intelligent sort of men than the ignorant peasants ... And the freeholders (say they) were not enslaved to their landlords as the tenants are. The gentry (say they) are wholly, by their estates and ambition, more dependent on the king than their tenants on them. ...

Thus he attributes greater economic and intellectual independence to the yeomanry and urban craftsmen than to those above or below them in the social scale, reinforcing the importance of social class. Where Clarendon attributed the attitude of the less substantial gentry and the middling-sort to envy or 'malignancy' towards their betters, Baxter points to the fear of upheaval and desire to preserve their power and possessions that motivated many supporters of the king. Again, there is other evidence to bear this out. Fear of disorder was a powerful motive among royalists as their 'party' took shape in 1641–2, and complaints about the breakdown of censorship, of radical preachers undermining the control exercised by the church, of public demonstrations and even enclosure riots were common throughout that year. It was no coincidence that the king's most effective propaganda came in his reply to the *Nineteen Propositions* when he argued that further changes in the constitution would 'destroy all rights and proprieties [property], all distinctions of families and merit, and by this means this splendid and excellently distinguished form of government [would] end in a dark, equal chaos of confusion'.

If class interest or ambition was one reason for the choosing of sides, another was religion. Clarendon referred to the 'factious' spirit among some urban corporations and the 'lecturers' that he mentions were the puritan preachers employed by many towns to hold week-day sermons, until this was forbidden by Laud. Baxter's conviction that religion was a decisive motivation is even stronger.

1   Though it must be confessed that the public safety and liberty wrought very much with most, especially with the nobility and gentry who adhered to the parliament; yet it was principally the differences about religious matters that filled up the parliament's armies, and put the
5   resolution and valour into their soldiers ... Not that the matter of Bishops or no Bishops was the main thing ... but the generality of the people through the land ... who were then called Puritans, ... religious persons that used to talk of God and Heaven and Scripture and holiness, and to follow sermons ... and speak against swearing, cursing,
10 drunkenness etc: I say the main body of this sort of men, both preachers and people, adhered to the parliament. And on the other side, the gentry that ... went to Church and heard Common Prayer ... and spoke against this [puritan] strictness and preciseness in religion ... the main body of these were against the parliament.

Again there is a great deal of evidence to support these contentions. Example after example could be cited of puritan volunteers for parliament, of parliamentarian troops destroying hated symbols of the Laudian régime like altar rails and surplices, of regiments listening to sermons and singing psalms in battle. Not all of these were of the 'middling-sort', but a significant proportion of the volunteers seem to have fitted this description. One such example is provided by Nehemiah Wharton, a sergeant in Lord Essex's army, who wrote to his master, Mr Willingham (indicating that Wharton had been

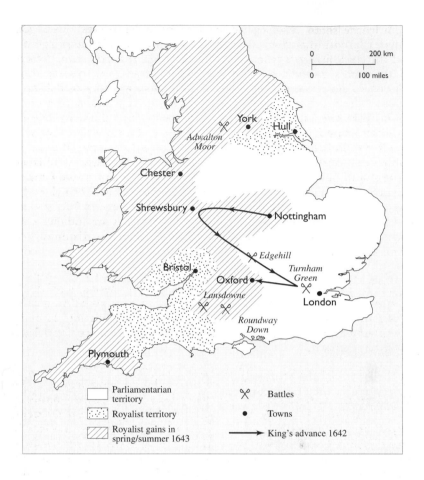

apprenticed or employed by Willingham and therefore fits the 'mid-dling' social category):

1 Wednesday: Mr Love gave us a famous sermon this day. Also, the soldiers brought the holy [altar] rails from Chiswick and burned them
   in our town. Thursday: I marched towards Uxbridge. And at
   Hillingdon, one mile from Uxbridge, the rails being gone, we got the
5 surplice to make us handkerchiefs; and one of the soldiers wore it to
   Uxbridge.

Religious motivation, however, spread through all classes.
Describing the situation in Nottinghamshire, Lucy Hutchinson
declared that 'the popish gentry were wholly for the king' while
the puritan Hutchinsons adhered to the parliamentary cause.
Their cousin,

1 Mr Henry Ireton ... having had an education in the strictest way of god-
liness ... was the chief promoter of the parliament's interest in the
county. But finding it generally disaffected, all he could do when the king
approached it was to gather a troop of those godly people which the
5 cavaliers drove out, and with them go into the army of my lord of Essex.

At the opposite end of the scale, Clarendon describes the intense
royalist feeling among the common people of Cornwall (despite 'a
wonderful and superstitious reverence towards the name of a parliament') because of their 'full submission and love of the established
government of Church and state, especially to that part of the Church
as concerned the liturgy, or Book of Common Prayer, which was a
most general object of veneration [respect] with the people'. In some
cases, puritan destruction of decorations and statues in local churches
caused great resentment, and the parliamentarian Thomas May
remarked that

1 some who were not bad men [were concerned about] the extreme
licence which the common people ... took to themselves of reforming
without authority, order or decency ... To this were added those daily
reports of ridiculous conventicles [meetings] and preachings made by
5 tradesmen and illiterate people of the lowest rank, to the scandal and
offence of many.

Whig historians argued that England divided in 1642 on the basis
of concerns about political liberty and religious conviction, while
Marxists emphasised class interest. The strong links between middling
and urban social groups and puritan convictions, and between
respect for the authority of king and Church and fear of social disorder, meant that belief and conviction often coincided with personal
and material interests. Both the central leadership whose commit-
ments were made in parliament during 1641 and 1642 and the
provincial supporters whose response emerged in the autumn of 1642
shared these common motivations. Hence, while the Whig and
Marxist interpretations of the causes of the Civil War are often seen
as conflicting, a detailed examination of the evidence suggests that
there were links between socio-economic status and religious preferences that make these interpretations compatible – they can, in fact,
be reconciled to offer a fuller and more balanced explanation.

b) Cross-currents and Complexities

A closer examination of the evidence, however, indicates that such
generalisations, while broadly accurate, are far too simplistic to offer
a sufficient explanation of the patterns of allegiance. Baxter and
Clarendon might agree on the broad social division of support, but
both indicate that members of the gentry did support the parliamentary cause. Numerous individuals fail to conform to the stereotypes

drawn above. In Derbyshire, the mainstay of the parliamentary cause was Sir John Gell, a great supporter of the Ship Money tax described by Lucy Hutchinson as 'a foul adulterer . . . and so unjust that without any remorse he suffered his men indifferently to plunder both honest men and cavaliers'. In his *History of the Parliament*, Thomas May describes the patterns of allegiance in terms which broadly agree with Clarendon and Baxter, but which also reveal some of the complex processes which went into the making of those patterns:

> ı In Suffolk, Norfolk, Cambridgeshire, Essex, Herts. Hunts. there was as much unanimity of opinion and affection in those counties . . . as was to be found in any part of England; but it was especially among the common people. For a great . . . number of the gentry, and those of
> 5 highest rank among them, were disaffected to the parliament . . . Which might have thrown those counties into as much distraction and sad calamity as any other part of the land had felt (if not wholly carried them to the other side). . . if those gentlemen had not been curbed and suppressed by that timely care which the parliament took, and more
> 10 particularly by the successful services of one gentleman, Mr Oliver Cromwell of Huntingdon. In the south-western counties [the Marquess of Hertford and Sir Ralph Hopton, commanding for the king] were both opposed . . . by private gentlemen of those counties.

What May indicates, and this can also be seen in the accounts by Clarendon and Baxter, is that divisions cut across most counties. Thus before the loyalty of the area was defined, an internal struggle occurred, and the outcome could be dictated by the actions of particular individuals and the influence of local or regional factors. In the south-eastern counties the proximity of London and parliament undoubtedly strengthened their cause, and as Baxter noted, the king never came there to help or stir up his sympathisers. Even so, the relative ease with which parliament controlled the area owed much to individuals like Cromwell. In the south-west and in Nottinghamshire, the parliamentarian gentry were in a minority, and could do little but surrender control of their county and move on to serve their cause elsewhere. As Lucy Hutchinson described it,

> ı Before the flame of the war broke out in the top of the chimneys, the smoke ascended in every country [county] . . . [and] in many places there were fierce contests and disputes (almost to blood) even at the first; for in the progress every county had the civil war (more or less)
> 5 within itself.

This evidence reveals the division of the nation as a gradual, piecemeal process, beginning before the official outbreak of hostilities and continuing for some months thereafter. Thus, local and regional struggles, with the exception of the Edgehill campaign, pre-occupied both sides in the winter of 1642–3. It is, moreover, increasingly clear that these struggles were essentially the work of committed minorities

rather than the county community as a whole. The difficulty of gen-
eralising about gentry reactions and motivations is illustrated by
Lawrence Stone in *The Causes of the English Revolution*, 1529–1642;

1 Despite the prodigious amount of research devoted to the subject in
   recent years, the motives for the alignments of the gentry when the war
   began are still not wholly clear ... [Socio-economic theories based on
   'rising gentry', 'lesser gentry', and 'declining gentry' have not proved
5 convincing in the light of the evidence]. Far more decisive than any
   socio-economic correlations is that with religion. In Yorkshire over one
   third of the Royalist gentry were Catholics, and over half of the
   Parliamentarians were Puritan ... All the Parliamentary leaders in
   Yorkshire had a previous record of strong Puritan sympathies.

What Stone shows is that religion can account for the allegiance of
something approaching half of the gentry and that it can explain the
behaviour of those who were most clearly and actively committed. Yet
if over half of the parliamentarian gentry in Yorkshire were puritans,
that still leaves a significant minority to be accounted for. Not all
counties divided on such clear religious lines. If fear of social
upheaval helps to explain why others chose the royalist cause, we are
still left with a substantial group of participants among the gentry
whose motives must have arisen from political considerations, or else
from other personal, local or random concerns.

Therefore, while political and religious motives remain significant
and valid as broad generalisations. Geography, the prevailing political
interest of the locality and the needs of survival must be taken into
account. In Lancashire the royalists quickly laid siege to parliamentarian Manchester and Bolton, and forcibly conscripted local men to fight
with them. The puritan minister Adam Martindale describes how his
brother tried to avoid the fighting until, faced with the threat of being
rounded up and marched off by the royalists, he went to Bolton and volunteered for the defence of the town. Thus some men were forced to
take one side, or pressurised to volunteer for the other. Few went as far
in trying to protect their lands and fortunes as the Earl of Kingston who,
according to Lucy Hutchinson, 'divided his sons between both parties
and concealed himself' until he was forced to make a choice, but it is
difficult to sustain the view that all, or even a large majority, of those
who fought made a conscious choice based on principle and belief as to
which side to support.

There are, moreover, many examples of men for whom conscience
and principle did not offer a clear choice. Throughout the spring and
summer of 1642 petitions poured in to king and parliament from all
parts of the country, almost universally demanding that they compose
their differences. Government by King-in-Parliament was the ideal of
the constitution, and government by the king under the law was the
desire of many who fought on both sides. A clear example of these
uncertainties and of the difficulties that they created is afforded by Sir

John Hotham, whose actions in securing Hull for the parliament were of crucial importance in the outcome of the war. Not only did this deny the king arms for 16,000 men, possession of the major supply port in the north of England and access to continental aid, but as a parliamentarian stronghold, Hull afforded refuge to the Fairfaxes in June 1643 and forced the Earl of Newcastle to delay his march south to join the king.

SIR JOHN HOTHAM

-Profile-

Hotham's actions could more accurately be described as reactions, and were certainly not the result of a coherent commitment and careful decision-making. In 1640–2 he supported the parliamentary opposition for both principled and personal reasons. He had opposed the collection of Ship Money and the billetting of soldiers in Yorkshire during the Bishops' Wars, and Charles had responded by insulting him and passing him over for appointment as governor of Hull. In January 1642 Hotham therefore accepted the nomination of parliament for the post, and seems to have been genuinely seeking to do his duty in this capacity when he refused the king access to the town in April of that year. Finding himself declared a traitor, he had little choice but to appeal to parliament for vindication. Thereafter he clearly had second thoughts and came close to surrendering the town in July 1642. In the winter of 1642–3 he quarrelled with the corporation, and made clear his dislike of the puritan influence among the Aldermen. Greatly concerned by the threat of popular disorder, he also became disillusioned with the parliamentary campaign, especially when the Fairfaxes were chosen to command the parliamentary forces rather than himself and his son. What finally tipped the balance seems to have been the Oxford negotiations; he blamed their failure upon the excessive demands of parliament. Thus in June 1643 Hotham agreed to hand Hull over to the royalists, but was prevented by local parliamentarians. Instead he was arrested and sent to London, where both he and his son, Captain Hotham, were executed as traitors in 1644. Hotham's case reveals the dilemmas facing those of moderate beliefs, the narrow margins that could separate royalist from parliamentarian, the personal or random elements that could dictate their final decisions, and the momentous influence that such factors could have on the outcome of events.

c) The Influence of Neutralism

The complications outlined above have been emphasised in recent research, which has focussed on local history and the study of how different county communities reacted to the looming shadow of war. What such studies also revealed was the importance of two other considerations in influencing the attitude of county communities to the growing conflict – the twin factors of neutralism and localism.

In 1642 every man was faced with a choice of sides – and many opted to choose no side at all. In the words of Clarendon, 'the number of these who desired to sit still was greater than of those who desired to engage in either party'. In Staffordshire the justices met to declare their county a neutral zone, in Cheshire and Yorkshire the royalist commissioners of array and the parliamentary militia commissioners (those who had been given the task of raising troops) made a mutual agreement not to proceed with their work in those counties. In Lincolnshire the gentry declared that they would not fight for or against the king, and raised a cavalry troop 'for the preservation of peace within themselves' and the defence of the county. In towns and boroughs the picture was much the same. Leicester shut its gates to all 'foreigners' and when the Earl of Bath came to South Molton in Devon to raise forces for the king, 'the common sort of the town fell in a great rage with the mayor and his company for giving licence that they should enter' and refused to allow the gentlemen to read their commission. Eventually they were attacked by the crowd 'some with muskets loaden, some with halberds and black bills [spears and axes], some with clubs ... The women had filled all the steps of the [market] cross with great stones, and got up and sat on them, swearing if they did come there they would brain them'. The commissioners beat a hasty retreat from the town.

Nor were these reactions in any way uncommon. In investigating this issue for his study *The Revolt of the Provinces*, John Morrill found attempted neutrality pacts in 22 English counties. As he described it

1 Fear [of disorder] drove some men into royalism; it drove far more into neutralism. Faced by the threat of social disintegration ... most counties closed ranks behind county barriers, determined (as they had been in the 1630s) to protect the administrative integrity of their shires as
5 the first line of defence against disorder.

These pacts fell into two broad categories. The first consists of agreements made between the royalist commissioners of array and the parliamentarian militia commissioners to cease recruitment in an effort to prevent bloodshed (or to conclude a truce once fighting had begun). It should perhaps be emphasised that both groups were usually native to the county in which they were expected to recruit, and would probably be well acquainted with one another. The second group involved more extensive and ambitious plans to exclude the war completely from particular areas, in which the local community not only refused to fight each other, but sought to raise a local force to prevent others from entering the area. Into this category came the agreements in Lincolnshire, Staffordshire, Cheshire and other counties in the summer and autumn of 1642, and the famous Cheshire 'Treaty of Bunbury' in December 1642. The situation was summarised by Derek Hirst in his study, *Authority and Conflict, 1603–1658*:

1   Everywhere, men sought an escape in neutralism. The ruin of Germany during the Thirty Years War, and the scattered agrarian unrest that had broken out all over the country in 1640–42 as political controls began to fracture, only reinforced the natural human pref-
5   erence for peace. Even those whose loyalties were clear, such as the parliamentarian Fairfaxes in Yorkshire, could recognise how much they had to lose and strove to neutralise their own areas – Sir John Hotham's fear lest 'the necessitous people ... set up for themselves to the utter ruin of the nobility and gentry' was widely shared. In county
10   after county gentlemen shunned both the militia ordinance and the commission of array.

The significance of these efforts to establish neutrality is threefold. In the first place they emphasise how undivided and uncommitted in many ways the country was. Far from rallying to either call and attacking their neighbours in pursuit of the cause to which they were dedicated, most of the gentry class, at least, seem to have reacted with uncertainty, confusion and fear. Secondly, they demonstrate the powerful fear of disorder which motivated many gentry efforts to keep the war from their doors. While this operated in general terms to the benefit of the royalists, it could equally persuade the county community to accept the presence of either army if they could guarantee that military presence would maintain order and control. Thirdly, they enhance the importance of the individuals and minorities, like Cromwell in the eastern counties and the Catholic gentry of Lancashire, who were committed to a cause and clear about their intentions. The 'civil war in every county' described by Lucy Hutchinson was in fact a battle between committed minorities, and the prize was the allegiance, or at least acceptance of the result, by the uncommitted majority.

Neutralism was not a permanent option. It characterised the reaction of many individuals to a situation that had got out of control, but once war had started, the demands of the committed parties for support, supplies and strategic advantage, would render the position of neutrals untenable. Neutrals would, in fact, be plundered by both sides. Hence the efforts at local treaties, which would afford some protection, and the attempts to organise local defence forces. In the end, as Hirst points out, they were doomed to failure, but they have a significance that goes beyond the simple human desire to avoid the danger and upheaval of war. What these neutralist treaties also reveal is the strength and importance of local and county communities, and the loyalties to them which have been labelled as 'localism'.

d) The Nature of Localism

Studies of county government and society in seventeenth-century England have provided clear evidence of what has been termed a localist perspective, emphasising the importance of the county community as an influence on outlook and behaviour. The treaties and agreements of the Civil War neutrals were not the work of individuals operating as independent units, but of community groups united by a shared perception of the locality and its needs. As Anthony Fletcher pointed out in studying *The Outbreak of the Civil War*, localism and neutralism were not exactly the same thing, although their effects could at times be similar. In many ways, seventeenth-century gentlemen belonged to their county first, and to their country second – indeed the word 'country' was more normally used at the time to describe a county or region than England as a whole. Although most gentlemen would spend a period of their youth at a university (Oxford and Cambridge were the only universities in England) and/or one of the Inns of Court in London, these were short interruptions of a life more normally spent in the management of an estate and the administration of local justice. Henry Oxinden, a Kentish gentleman, visited London once in his lifetime, while Mary Hyde, the mother of the future Lord Clarendon, never once left her native county of Wiltshire. For most of the gentry families, their county community, united by ties of blood, marriage and interest, and divided by local rivalries and issues more than national concerns, was the primary political unit. In the words of Alan Everitt, 'In some respects the England of 1640 resembled a union of partially independent states, rather as Canada today is a union of self-governing provinces, or America of federated states: and that union, as we all know, is not always a very simple or easy relationship' [*The Local Community and the Great Rebellion*, p. 8].

This did not mean that the members of these county communities had no views about the national issues of King, Church and Parliament, nor that localism was equally powerful in all places and for all individuals. While counties such as Yorkshire, Cornwall and even Kent (for all its proximity to London) had strong and fairly self-contained communities, others like Warwickshire were more open and diffuse. Nevertheless, localism was a significant factor in much of the country, and its significance lies in its capacity to complicate the division of loyalties that occurred in 1642. A local perspective could influence decisions in a number of ways. In the first place, concern for the well-being of the local area could influence the willingness of individuals to participate fully in the struggle. In Kent, Alan Everitt found that the majority of the gentry, moderate royalists and parliamentarians alike, were reluctant to participate in the struggle, which was essentially fought out by opposing minorities, many of whom had connections outside the county. Secondly, it could affect the choice of whom to support. In Staffordshire the neutrality pact was eventually abandoned in favour of the royalists, not because there were no parliamentarian sympathisers, but because the royalists were better-placed to assist in preventing lower-class disorders and preserve the peace of the county. Thirdly, localism could influence the taking of sides through the existence of local rivalries, particularly among those who were torn between conflicting beliefs and for whom the choice was therefore difficult. One clear example of this lies in the behaviour of Sir John Hotham, whose initial support of parliament was encouraged by dislike of the Wentworth influence in Yorkshire, and whose attempt to join the royalists in 1643 was equally motivated by rivalry with the Fairfaxes. This point is reinforced by John Morrill, who showed in his *Revolt of the Provinces* that 'pre-existent power groupings within each county' had a good deal of influence on the taking of sides.

The overall effect of localism, therefore, is to complicate the task of deciding and describing how England divided in 1642; and this makes especially dangerous any attempt to draw upon this material to explain either the causes or the significance of the outbreak of war. We cannot simply catalogue the actions that men took in choosing sides, or not, and make inferences from this about the extent and strength of support that each side enjoyed, let alone draw conclusions as to why. As Anthony Fletcher explained 'It is hard to believe . . . that many well-informed men were pure neutrals at heart. The leading men in the shires, and to some extent the same goes for mayors and aldermen, had been too much involved in the political debate to avoid adopting their own standpoints. Few surely saw a precisely equal amount of right on both sides. Yet at the same time everyone who was politically aware faced the dilemma that by being true to their deepest feelings they might increase polarisation and destroy local peace. Thus commitment and activism were not the same things' [*The Outbreak of the English Civil War*, p. 380]. Some men were committed but reluctant to take action, others active, but for motives other than a straightforward commitment; and some, perhaps a majority, simply tried to balance their conflicting loyalties they best way they could.

e) The Loyalties of the People

Thus far, consideration has been given to the reactions of the social and political leaders – the gentry and the borough corporations – but any conclusions about the nature of divisions in England must also address the role and opinions of the common people of the time. It is difficult to assess the strength and nature of popular feeling in these circumstances, because the views of the ordinary citizen or peasant farmer were so rarely recorded. However, David Underdown and Derek Hirst have both been able to show that awareness of political issues extended well down the social scale. According to Underdown in his *Revel, Riot and Rebellion,* 'There is, in fact, plentiful evidence that ... ordinary Englishmen had opinions on national issues that reflected their underlying concern for law, custom and 'good rule''. He argues that the nature of these concerns and their tendency to see the issues in local terms differs little from the attitudes displayed by the ruling elites. One source of evidence about popular attitudes can be found in the Quarter Sessions records, of prosecutions for seditious or insulting words. The records for Exeter in October–November 1642, for example, reveal a threat to poison the Prince of Wales who was resident nearby, a threat to open the town gates to the king's forces, and the singing of lewd songs about the king, the queen and the Earl of Manchester. Most of these incidents seem to have occurred in the various ale-houses of the city, but they probably serve to reveal genuine feeling even if there was little likelihood of the threats being carried out.

In so far as it is possible to interpret such scanty evidence, it would appear that ordinary citizens were indeed aware of the issues involved in the Civil War, although not necessarily able to make free decisions about how to respond to them. According to contemporary commentators many tenants were expected or forced to follow the leadership of their lords; while independent craftsmen seem to have followed the cause of parliament. In neither case is it possible to generalise too freely. In boroughs such as Hull and Gloucester the decision about whom to support was made by the governor (if there was one) and corporation – but once made it was apparently widely accepted. Certainly the ordinary citizens of these towns played an active part in resisting royalist attacks. This may have arisen from respect for the town's governing body, from habits of accepting their authority, from genuine commitment, or from a mixture of all three. Equally likely, the requirements of survival may have dictated that the town should pull together in defence of home and property. The fate of towns which were taken by storm, or surrendered after a siege was not such as to encourage defenders to give up easily; plunder and looting were considered the soldiers' due. When Beverley surrendered without resistance to the royalist army as it approached Hull, their town was sacked and partly burned. The lesson would not have been lost on the citizens of Hull, who fought determinedly for the following three months to prevent the Earl of Newcastle from capturing the town. Indeed the most reasonable conclusion about the views of ordinary citizens is that they reacted in exactly the same ways as others – some volunteered on principle, some sympathised with the king and some with parliament, most were concerned with local needs and consequences, and ultimately, they sought to survive and protect what they had.

This evidence also suggests that, however the decisions of 1642–3 were taken, they were difficult to reverse. A town that surrendered would be liable to damage and destruction, no less than one which was taken by force. The experience of individuals who sought to change sides was not encouraging, as Hotham discovered. The Earls of Bedford, Holland and Clare, who left parliament in protest at the Scottish alliance of 1643, found themselves less than welcome at the Court of a king who sought victory rather than peace. When armies were defeated, it was common practice for both sides to recruit the rank and file into their own forces, but this was more difficult for the higher ranks. For the most part, the division of the country became more effective as the war progressed, as both sides established administrative and military committees in the areas under their control. By mid-1643 the division of the nation had become a fact with which those who were thus divided had to live as best they could.

3 Assessment; A Nation Divided?

The argument above began with an account of the processes, issues and motivations that divided the nation between king and parliament, but the evidence provided thereafter raises serious doubts about how far this concept of clear-cut division can be accepted as valid. In the autumn and winter of 1642–3 there is evidence of widespread neutralism and a reluctance to participate; in many areas the gentry joined ranks to protect their county community, whose needs and interests were at least as important as those of the two main protagonists. Their efforts were doomed to failure, but the initial division of the country into royalist and parliamentarian areas had to be conducted through these county communities and with their agreement. This was to complicate the process and ultimately to allow committed minorities to seize the initiative and direct the decisions of the more uncertain majority. In these circumstances, individual, geographical, and sometimes random, factors could have considerable influence upon the outcome, and their effects could be difficult to reverse.

In the end, war did occur, and was sustained for several years. What Derek Hirst called 'fortress Staffordshire' and the other counties did fall to one side or the other. Individuals chose to raise regiments for their cause, and there is evidence that hundreds, if not thousands, of men freely volunteered to fight. For a minority, an intensely committed minority, there were simple choices. On both sides there were those who knew where their priorities lay, and who acted quickly and decisively in pursuit of those priorities. On the royalist side, they were mainly fighting in defence of the king and the existing structure of society, in fear of the aspirations and ambitions of the lower orders, and sometimes through affection and respect for the Anglican Church. On the parliamentarian side there was loyalty to the parliament and the rule of law that it represented, fear of a royal tyranny that would deprive the individual of his rights and privileges, and above all, religious commitment – to Protestantism in its more radical forms, or at least to the defeat of popery. Among those for whom these choices were stark, there was a clear division. For the majority, however, there were divided loyalties – to king and to parliament, to the rule of law and the existing hierarchy, to the Protestant religion and the traditions of the Church, and above all, to the nation and the local community. In many ways the nation did not so much divide as fragment, with the fragments held together in two camps by war and necessity.

Summary Diagram
Summary – A Nation Divided, 1642–3

King	Geographical loyalties	Parliament
West, South-west and Wales	Yorkshire/Midlands split and divided	London and South-east

Pull Factors	Class loyalties	Pull Factors
Social hierarchy	Aristocracy ----▶	Social ambitions
Catholic/Anglican	Gentry ----▶	Puritanism
Rural attitudes and structure	Middling sort (yeomen and craftsmen)	Urban attitudes and structure
Court influence	Tenantry (rural)	London influence
	Others?	

Cross-currents and complexities

Geographical proximity of main armies and strategic centres

Localism and Neutralism

Interaction of different and competing 'pull' factors

Individual/personal considerations and rivalries

◀──▶   ◀──▶   ◀──▶   ◀──▶   ◀──▶   ◀──▶

Working on Chapter 3

The structure of the chapter is fairly straightforward, and for the purposes of note-making it can be taken one section at a time. The first section provides a chronological account of the process of division, and notes made in reasonable detail will provide an account of the first year of the war. Thereafter the approach is analytical, with each section focusing on a particular issue. Overall, your notes should allow you to explain how the country gradually took sides in the first year of war, what factors motivated individuals in making their choices, the reluctance with which many made such choices, and the problems involved in drawing any general conclusions or inferences about the causes of the war.

Source-based questions on Chapter 3

While essay questions on this topic are unlikely to be asked at AS or A level, there is a rich supply of sources for source-based questions. There is considerable variation in the nature and importance of the source-based questions used by the different examination boards, and you should try to collect and practise answering examples from past papers which are specific to the examination that you will take. However, the skills that are being tested do fall into two broad categories. The first relates to the ability to understand sources – testing comprehension, understanding of language, inference and deduction, and the ability to cross-reference and use sources together. The second builds on these essential skills by asking you to interpret and assess the significance of sources in a wider context, considering how far a source is reliable, typical or representative, and how far particular sources can be used as a basis for wider conclusions and generalisations. Practice in using these skills separately has already been provided at the end of Chapter 2. However, an historical investigation such as that demonstrated in this chapter requires you to both integrate them, and to apply them for a particular purpose. To practise this higher level source handling you should:

1. Re-read Chapter 3. As you work through the author's commentary on the sources, identify:
   - statements that you consider to show comprehension, analysis, interpretation, evaluation and cross-referencing;
   - statements and stages that build up an argument by linking different information;
   - statements that use contextual knowledge to develop the ideas/arguments based on the sources;
   - statements that synthesise the material into wider conclusions.

2. Using the sources from Clarendon and Baxter on pp. 61–3 [3–5] and your own knowledge, construct an argument to show how far England divided along class lines in 1642–3.

4 The Victory of Parliament, 1643–6

POINTS TO CONSIDER

By 1643 the division of England into two sides was virtually complete, and the failure of the peace negotiations at Oxford indicated that, unless the King could use his initial advantages to snatch victory in the 1643 campaign, there would be a long and costly conflict. Chapter 4 sets out to explain why he was unable to achieve this victory, and why in 1646 he was forced to surrender and admit defeat. As you work through the chapter, therefore, you should be looking to establish the causal factors that explain his defeat, and the process by which they combined and interacted to bring it about.

KEY DATES

1643	June	Parliament signed the Solemn League and Covenant with the Scots.
	July	Royalists captured Bristol.
	September	Essex lifted the royalist siege of Gloucester and the king's advance on London was held at Newbury.
	October	Royalist siege of Hull broken.
		King signed the Cessation [truce] with the Irish rebels.
	December	Assembly of Divines [ministers] met in Westminster.
		Death of Pym.
1644	February	Committee of Both Kingdoms established to run the war for Parliament.
	July	Battle of Marston Moor and surrender of York secured parliamentary control of the north.
	August	Essex surrendered in Cornwall and quarrels among parliamentary generals allowed the royalists to escape at the second battle of Newbury.
	December	Self-Denying Ordinance passed by Parliament.
1645	January	Committee of Both Kingdoms agreed the formation of a New Model Army.
	June	Battle of Naseby.
	September	Prince Rupert surrendered Bristol and Montrose was defeated in Scotland.
1646	March/April	Gradual surrender of remaining royalist forces in the south-west. The king left Oxford in disguise on April 27.
	May 5	King surrendered to the Scots at Southwell, Notts. and moved north with them to Newcastle.

Introduction: The Victory of Parliament

KEY ISSUE Why did Parliament win the Civil War of 1642–6?

By the summer of 1643 the war appeared to be going the way of the king. After Prince Rupert's capture of Bristol (see p. 60) the royalists were able to consolidate their hold on the west and link up the south-western counties with the royalist heartland of South Wales and the neighbouring districts in England. In August, Maurice captured Dorchester, gaining control of Dorset, and followed this up in September by taking Exeter. Only in Gloucester and Plymouth did sizeable parliamentarian garrisons hold out, and Gloucester at least seemed vulnerable to siege. In the north the royalists held most of the north-eastern counties and Newcastle's victory over the Fairfaxes at Adwalton Moor in June had secured control of Yorkshire. Only Hull, where the arrest of Hotham had retained the town for parliament and allowed the Fairfaxes to take refuge, still held out. There appeared to be little to prevent the king from carrying out his strategy of linking up his northern and western armies with his own at Oxford, and moving on towards London. With a respect for the London trained bands learned the previous year at Turnham Green, he intended to blockade the city and look to a rising of the citizens to bring about its fall. Nor was this an unlikely outcome, given the distress caused by parliamentary taxes and the increased hardship that such a blockade would create. Yet the march on London never came, and three years later, his options and resources exhausted, the king was forced to surrender. That he chose to surrender to the Scots rather than to parliament is evidence of his reluctance to admit defeat; but the overwhelming military superiority of parliament gave him no choice.

How, then, are we to explain such a remarkable change in the fortunes of the two protagonists? The answer lies in a combination of factors. For a variety of reasons, the king was unable to capitalise upon his early advantages. Secondly, the position of parliament was not as disastrous as it appeared, and included certain long-term advantages if survival could be secured for long enough to capitalise on them. That this occurred owed much to the tactical genius of John Pym. Thirdly, the needs and demands of war brought harder and more radical leaders to the fore in both camps, and this ultimately led to a military revolution in which parliament finally concentrated its considerable resources into a single, mobile and highly effective fighting force. In the end, it was the New Model Army which brought about a military victory for parliament. Ironically, its creation, its successes and its ideals made the task of establishing a political settlement thereafter, far more difficult.

1 The Failure of the Royalists

> **KEY ISSUES** Why was Charles unable to achieve victory in
> 1643–4? Was Charles an inadequate leader?

The king's position as monarch gave him a number of advantages in
the early months of the war. He was able to call upon the loyalty of
many of the gentry, and thus to acquire both money and skilled horse-
men for his cavalry. The Earl of Worcester, for example, donated in
the region of £300,000 before the war was over. According to Derek
Hirst in his study of *Authority and Conflict, 1603–58*, the vast majority of
the professional officer corps, many of whom were serving abroad in
1642, returned to serve the king. He was also able to call upon the
support of foreign rulers, particularly his relatives in the United
Provinces who had experience of war and abundant supplies of
cavalry horses. Unlike parliament, he had a unified command and a
clear strategy. For all of these reasons, he was able to organise and
mobilise effective forces far more quickly than his opponents; the results
were shown in the Edgehill campaign and in his early successes in 1643.

Historians have argued that these royalist advantages were dissipated by a failure of leadership, in which a hesitant king failed to
develop an effective administration or to control his commanders
adequately, so that the royalist war effort became fragmented. In
some cases his more ruthlessly military commanders alienated local
populations by allowing indiscriminate plunder, which contrasted
with the discipline and restraint of the parliamentary troops.
Eventually, the argument goes, neutrals and local resistance groups
were driven to the side of parliament. As with many simple explanations, the argument contains valid elements and partial truths, but
is by no means the whole story.

In many ways the royalist war effort followed the same pattern as
that of parliament. In both cases recruiting by commissioners was
resisted, and both sides relied initially on volunteers who raised individual regiments and troops from among their friends, neighbours
and tenants. Later, both sides began, with some trepidation, forcibly
to conscript for their armies. Where parliament placed county administration in the hands of the Lords Lieutenant, the king appointed six
Lieutenant-Generals to administer the counties under royalist control. Co-ordination was provided by a Council of War at Oxford, similar to parliament's Committee of Safety. In both cases those
appointed were chosen for their social and political status rather than
their military or administrative expertise. In the light of experience,
both sides became more efficient and more ruthless in their methods.
By mid-1643 Charles had replaced early commanders such as the
Marquess of Hertford with military leaders such as his nephews,
Rupert and Maurice, and had begun to levy local rates in co-operation

with civilian county committees similar to those of parliament. It is undoubtedly the case that these rates caused friction and were often in arrears. It is also true that they were sometimes forcibly collected, in kind, and that some commanders, such as Goring in Somerset, allowed local communities to be plundered regardless of their loyalties. Yet these problems were less a result of faults in the system than of the sheer weight and quantity of demands for supplies once the war passed its initial stages.

More accurate is the charge that Charles failed to control the conflicting aims and ambitions of his commanders and advisers. At certain times royalist strategy lacked direction, and in 1643 the failure of the northern and western armies to link up with Charles at Oxford destroyed what was probably the king's best chance of outright victory. Although there were rivalries involved, notably between Prince Rupert and Digby, the delay in the royalist advance also arose from military considerations. In Yorkshire, the Earl of Newcastle was reluctant to advance south while leaving a parliamentary force in Hull to harry his rear; he may also have been concerned by a threat of intervention from Scotland. The western forces were similarly delayed by the sieges of Gloucester and Plymouth. Newcastle has been criticised for his decision, particularly as Hull's position and parliament's naval strength made the town difficult to besiege successfully, but both Hull and Gloucester did constitute a threat to vital supply lines. As it was, the king himself began the siege of Gloucester in August and the town was relieved by Essex in September. When the king tried to prevent Essex's return to London, he was defeated at the battle of Newbury on 20 September. Thereafter, a successful attack on London was unlikely, and he withdrew to Oxford. Three weeks later Fairfax broke the siege of Hull, and a few days later the success of Cromwell and Fairfax at Winceby in Lincolnshire secured control of the Humber estuary and its southern bank. Newcastle therefore abandoned the siege on the same day, 11 October.

While there is no doubt of the importance of these failures, and that royalist rivalries were partially responsible for the priority given to the regional campaigns, it cannot be said that failures of leadership on the part of the king were entirely, or perhaps even mainly responsible. More serious was the division within the royalist ranks over the ultimate objectives of the fighting. While Edward Hyde and the moderates sought to find a negotiated settlement, and to win over moderate opinion, it was increasingly clear that the king aimed at military victory and listened most closely to the advice of the queen, militarists like Rupert, and the extremist Lord Digby. In 1643 when the moderate Lord Falkland was killed in the fighting, he was replaced by Digby as Secretary of State. Thus, while the king delayed the levying of a county rate until 1643, and sought to maintain legal forms in order to placate local opinion, he increasingly undid the effect of this by the influence given to militarist advisers. The clearest example of these errors came in the autumn of 1643 when he retaliated against parliament's Scottish alliance by agreeing a Cessation (truce) with the Catholic rebels in Ireland. His purpose was to free the experienced English troops engaged in Ireland in order to use them himself, but given contemporary attitudes towards the Irish, he granted his opponents an enormous propaganda victory. Rumours of Irish Catholic troops and Irish atrocities in England abounded. More immediately, the carefully laid plans constructed by Hyde to capitalise on anti-Scottish sentiment, both within and outside parliament, were swept aside by the spate of anti-Catholic feeling and the apparent confirmation that the king was conspiring with Irish Catholic rebels.

It is true, therefore, that royalist administration was imperfect, that royalist strategy was uncertain and that the royalist leadership was, at times, divided. Nevertheless, these failings were mirrored by their opponents, whose weaknesses, uncertainties and divisions were as great or greater than those in the royalist camp. What made the royalist weaknesses so much more damaging were two factors – first, that they had fewer resources and long-term advantages to squander, and secondly, that the effect of parliament's weaknesses was minimised by the work and achievements of John Pym. The fact was that the counties under royalist control, the north, south-west and west midlands, were poorer than the parliamentarian south-east, and the midland counties were also the scene of constant fierce fighting. Parliamentary garrisons such as that at Gloucester were not only strategically important, but were also able to harry and harass the countryside upon which the royal armies depended. With parliament in control of the navy and of most of the major ports, the king was never able to make full use of his foreign allies. The cavaliers who left their estates in order to serve the king were increasingly less able to bear the burdens of financing him. In short, the king's strengths and advantages were most valuable for a short war and a rapid strike – and once that had failed, the advantage would slowly move towards parliament.

In these circumstances, the royalist failings took on a more crucial importance. The king did build up a more effective military and administrative system, but the delay was costly. Individual errors of strategy in 1643 were damaging because they wasted diminishing opportunities. However, this did not mean that a parliamentarian victory became inevitable thereafter. What was so crucial about the royalists' failures in 1642–3 was that they allowed the parliament to survive its darkest hours, and to begin to utilise the resources at its disposal. In the long run these were greatly superior to their own.

2 The Assets of Parliament

a) Parliament and its Problems

The strengths and weaknesses of the parliamentary cause were almost exactly opposite to those of the king. Where the king had a unified command and administration, parliament had to rely on a series of overlapping committees, whose ability to initiate new and more efficient systems was limited. Reliance upon county and local militias made military planning even more difficult, and only in the moments of greatest danger did the county committees overcome local concerns and effectively pool their resources. They did, however, maintain links with local support, which proved to be of benefit in the long run in preventing some of the military abuses that created anti-royalist feeling in counties such as Somerset. Control of the navy was of great strategic importance, especially in the long-term, and the resources of the parliamentary heartland in the south-east were substantial once the means of drawing on them was established.

The political divisions that beset the royalists were magnified within a parliament of nearly two hundred, many of whom were, and remained, backbench MPs with limited appreciation of what war would involve. While many were capable of contributing, time and experience were required. The more influential members fell into three main groups. The 'peace party' was led by a number of Lords and by Denzil Holles in the Commons and had strictly limited and defensive war aims. The 'war party', led by Sir Henry Vane, Sir Arthur Haselrig and the republican Henry Marten, openly sought the total defeat of the king as a prelude to severely reducing his powers. Linking and organising these forces were a middle group led by Pym, with the help of Oliver St. John, John Hampden and Oliver Cromwell, who sought a negotiated settlement which would include control over the armed forces and the king's advisers. The purpose, and achievement, of this group was to hold together this fragile coalition while developing the measures needed to fight a war. While the king needed to strike and act quickly, the parliamentary cause would require time to organise, develop, and tap its considerable resources.

b) The Role of Pym

KEY ISSUE How did Pym lay the foundations for victory?

That this time was found and used constructively was due, in no small measure to the leadership of John Pym. In the first year of the war his greatest achievements lay in two areas – his ability to utilise the dangers and disasters of the military situation to persuade conservative MPs to adopt radical measures, and his ability to hold together the peace and war parties despite their conflicting aims. Thus he used the failure at Edgehill and Rupert's assault on Brentford to persuade MPs to establish compulsory weekly assessments (taxes) in London, which were later extended to other areas. By persuading parliament thus to assume powers of taxation, extended by the introduction of an excise tax after the breakdown of peace negotiations at Oxford in the spring of 1643, he laid the basis of a reasonably effective financial structure. In December 1642 he was able to reduce localist obstruction, at least a little, by establishing the Midland and Eastern Associations to co-ordinate county administration and military effort. Nevertheless, the benefits of these measures would take time to be felt, and in the meantime, royalist success threatened to make them irrelevent. Royalist delays, the determined resistance of Hull and Gloucester, and the unexpected success of the Eastern Association armies, along with Essex's victory at Newbury, saved parliament that summer. Pym utilised the time given, as well as the fears aroused, to introduce a new strategy – an alliance with the battle-hardened army of the Scottish Covenanters.

While such a strategy might well seem obvious, to contemporaries it was both dangerous and unwelcome. The Scots rebels had enabled the opposition in the Long Parliament to challenge Charles, but they were far from popular in England. To long standing anti-Scottish sentiment could be added a dislike of the rigid brand of Presbyterianism adopted by the Scottish Kirk, even among those of Puritan sympathies, and there was no doubt that a religious settlement of this kind would be the price of Scottish support. To many of the moderates, this had another disadvantage – it would make a negotiated settlement with the king even harder to achieve, since his genuine devotion to the Anglican Church would not allow him to accept a Presbyterian settlement. The specific association of the parliamentary cause with Presbyterian reform in the Church threatened their hopes of peace, and tied them to an obligation for which many moderates had little liking. By bringing in another party who might well claim a place at any negotiating table, Pym was complicating the process and reducing its chances of success. By bringing the Scots into the armed conflict, he was also widening the scope of war and changing its character. To those who sought a peace based on minimising differences with the royalists and reaching a rapid compromise, the Scottish Covenanters and their religious crusade appeared to be disastrous allies.

With considerable skill Pym met these difficulties and pushed his strategy through. He avoided a total commitment to Scottish Presbyterianism by agreeing to call an Assembly of Ministers to devise a scheme of reform. The details of this scheme were to be settled 'as may be agreeable to God's Holy Word' – a form of words which both pre-empted criticism and invited months, if not years, of debate before any final decisions could be made. He blocked a new peace initiative on the basis that, given parliament's weakness at this time, the only negotiation that the king would accept would be their surrender. Shortly afterwards, however, he secured the expulsion of the republican Henry Marten from the Commons, in a move that reassured many of the peace party, as well as removing the most aggressive leader of the war party. Finally, Charles himself sealed Pym's success in holding together the parliamentary coalition by agreeing a truce with the Irish rebels [the Irish Cessation], and raising once more the menace of popery.

Therefore, when Pym died in December 1643 he had steered the parliamentary cause through its most difficult period and had laid the base for future development. The military situation was one of stalemate, but parliament had acquired a powerful ally whose value would be shown in the following year. The system of administration was adequate, and the financial reforms of the spring were at last beginning to bear fruit. With the rich south-eastern counties securely under control, the support of the navy and the Scottish alliance, those who took over Pym's role had at least the basic material for success.

3 The Achievement of Victory

> **KEY ISSUE** How did Parliament's forces avoid defeat and achieve victory?

a) Marston Moor: a Victory for Co-operation?

> **KEY ISSUE** In what ways was the battle of Marston Moor a turning-point in Parliament's fortunes?

That success was by no means assured or automatic. Although Pym had persuaded parliament to accept the Scottish alliance, stresses and tensions remained, to which the Scots themselves contributed by their continuing efforts to obtain the establishment of a Presbyterian Church in England. In the spring of 1644 St. John and Vane, supported by Lord Saye and Sele in the Lords, succeeded in reducing the power of the peace party by re-organising the parliamentary administration. The old Committee of Safety was replaced by a Committee of Both Kingdoms upon which the war and middle parties were more strongly represented. Unfortunately this offended the military commander, the Earl of Essex, especially when the committee diverted some resources to the armies of Manchester and Waller in the south-east. Although Manchester's Eastern Association army was already proving the most effective of the parliamentary forces, its value was undermined by a localist outlook which limited its sphere of operations. While the Scots army remained in the north, besieging the city of Newcastle, the parliamentary forces in the south squabbled, failed to co-ordinate, and suffered a serious defeat at Cropredy Bridge in Oxfordshire in June 1644. Beset by political and military divisions at the centre, the parliamentary cause was rescued by one of its more peripheral associations – the Yorkshire armies led by Fairfax.

The retreat to Hull in 1643 and the successful resistance against Newcastle's siege had given the Yorkshire army the opportunity to regroup. In January 1644 Sir Thomas Fairfax had destroyed the biggest contingent of Charles's Irish forces (released by the Cessation) at Nantwich in Cheshire, before turning east to link up with the Scots. By April Fairfax had succeeded, with the help of a Scottish contingent, in forcing Newcastle's army back into York, where they were now besieged. Realising the strategic importance of his northern army, and of York itself, Charles sent Prince Rupert to relieve the city – a mission in which he was successful. Unfortunately, however, Rupert then chose to meet the parliamentary forces in open battle, despite the fact that Manchester and Cromwell had now brought the Eastern Association army to reinforce Fairfax and the Scots, and bring the parliamentary total to 28,000 men. On 2 July the armies clashed at Marston Moor, and after a fierce struggle, the royalist army was broken. York surrendered two weeks later.

The battle of Marston Moor was of enormous significance in the war, yet its military importance was less than might have been expected. Certainly it secured the north for parliament, and reduced royalist control to its western heartlands, but there were some strategic advantages in a geographically compact military base. Moreover, beset by internal differences, the parliamentary forces failed to follow up their military advantage. It is even possible that the success of his rivals actually goaded the discontented Essex into his most disastrous error – a march west in search of an equally spectacular victory against the king's western armies. He succeeded in relieving the besieged Lyme, in Dorset, but then allowed himself to be trapped in the southwestern peninsula, eventually abandoning his entire army in Cornwall. Thereafter the victorious royalists turned east, to be met at Newbury in Berkshire by a reluctant and internally divided force from the Eastern Association. The indecisive battle that followed allowed the King and his force to return safely to Oxford. Militarily the situation had ended once more in stalemate, and the gains of Marston Moor had been dissipated.

Politically, however, the battle was to have far-reaching effects in bringing to the surface the underlying tensions and differences that divided the parliamentary movement. The political differences between the peace and war parties partly reflected, and were certainly complicated by, religious issues which the Scottish presence helped to intensify. Few conservative parliamentarians were committed to any form of Presbyterianism, least of all the Scottish model, but they were concerned about order and social discipline, and regarded a national Church based on authority and compulsion as essential in maintaining such controls. From the time of the collapse of censorship in 1641, they had been concerned at the spate of radical pamphlets and activities of religious separatists which had been permitted, and which had increased with the outbreak of war. Nowhere had these enthusiasts found a more sympathetic response than in the army of the Eastern Association, where both Cromwell and Manchester had sought to recruit men of religious zeal and commitment to the cause. Moreover, when such men distinguished themselves by their effort and dedication, they were promoted in the name of efficiency and military effectiveness. These policies had contributed a great deal to success of the Eastern Association, particularly in creating a cavalry whose courage matched, and whose discipline outshone, the royalists. It was Cromwell's cavalry which tipped the balance at Marston Moor when, unlike Rupert's successful forces on the other wing of the battle, it had sufficient discipline to regroup and attack the royalist centre to destroy Newcastle's infantry. The problem for the more cautious parliamentarians was that militarily they needed such men, while politically they feared them.

By raising the issue of the future organisation of the Church, the Scottish alliance had crystallised such fears. When separatist demands for a measure of religious toleration emerged within the Assembly of Divines itself, concern grew, complaints multiplied, and Manchester's Scottish Major-General, Crawford, sought to reassert control within the Eastern Association army. His attempts to purge separatist officers and discipline soldiers for preaching in the place of ordained ministers had already led to bitter quarrels with Cromwell before Marston Moor, but the battle increased tensions in several ways. When Cromwell and others saw at first hand the rigid Presbyterianism of the Scots, they were confirmed in their determination to oppose it. When victory came through their efforts rather than those of the Scots, they were confirmed in their conviction that they had God's approval; and when conservatives, Scottish and English alike, saw the effectiveness of Cromwell's 'godly party' they determined to reduce their power and number.

It was in this context that a bitter power struggle broke out within the parliamentarian ranks, in which the competing and overlapping aims of three parties created a confusion of shifting factions and enmities. In parliament the middle group was already finding itself closer to the so-called war party. Within the army of the Eastern Association, open feuding occurred between the supporters of Cromwell and the Presbyterian officers, in which each side promoted men of their own persuasion and sought to purge their opponents. Manchester was unable to control the effects of this squabbling, and the military results were seen in the failure at Newbury. When the war party in the Commons attacked Essex, the peace group and the

Presbyterians were able to counter-attack at the expense of Cromwell. Manchester himself seems to have become convinced of the futility of the struggle against the king, declaring that 'if we fight a hundred times and beat him ninety and nine times, he will be king still ... But if he beat us but once, or the last time, we shall be hanged.' When the crisis came to a head, he aligned himself with the conservatives. In imminent danger of political defeat, Cromwell and his allies in parliament outflanked their opponents with the introduction of the *Self-denying Ordinance* in December 1644.

The Ordinance admitted fault on all sides, and proposed a separation of military and political functions which would create a new, central army led by military men. It would thus remove all members of parliament from within this army and allow it to function without political interference. It had the attraction of providing a military reorganisation which all parties could see the need for, and a solution to the political deadlock in which the parliamentarians were trapped. As members of the House of Lords, the old generals would lose their places, without personal humiliation. Since the main purpose of the war party was to win the war, this in itself would serve their aims. The Ordinance was quickly accepted by the Commons, but met with stiff opposition in the Lords whose members would be the greatest losers. However, while the Lords wrangled, proof of the need for a military victory came from the king at Oxford. Under pressure from the Scots new negotiations had been opened, with parliamentary and Scottish commissioners meeting the king at Uxbridge. Not only did Charles reiterate his old position, but the Scottish insistence on a Presbyterian Church opened new disputes (see Appendix). By January 1645 it was clear that a negotiated settlement was as far away as ever, and the Lords had little choice but to accept the Ordinance. Thereafter, attention turned to the appointment of its leading officers. The Lord General was Sir Thomas Fairfax, a man of moderate Puritan convictions and good military reputation. His Major-General of the Infantry was Philip Skippon, another moderate who had led the London Trained Bands to victory at Turnham Green in 1642. No Lieutenant-General of the Horse could be agreed upon by the Lords, and so at last Fairfax requested that he be served by Oliver Cromwell on a temporary basis, until agreement could be reached.

The outcome could hardly have been better for the war party. Cromwell continued to serve on a series of three month commissions and was able to contribute his considerable abilities to the formation of a new and highly effective fighting force. The New Model Army did not spring into being immediately as a military miracle. It was based upon existing regiments, many of its officers were gentlemen of social status, and many of the rank and file were pressed men or professional soldiers interested only in their pay. Nevertheless it had great advantages over its predecessors. It was for the most part fairly well paid, it was well-drilled and disciplined, and it was not attached to any regional location. One of the main reasons for the speed with which the New Model was to mop up the remaining royalist forces in 1645–6 was the rapidity with which it could move, bringing its full force to bear upon an enemy whose forces remained divided and fragmented. Perhaps most important of all, the core of the New Model came from the old army of the Eastern Association and carried over the principles of promotion by merit, religious enthusiasm and godly discipline that had begun to make that army such a formidable fighting unit. In the short term the military advantages of this were significant; in the long term the political effects would be even more so.

b) The Victory of the New Model Army

> **KEY ISSUES** How did the New Model Army contribute to military victory? How important were the errors of the royalists?

For the moment the military issue was paramount, and it is ironic that the first major success of the New Model Army was to be provided in many ways by the king. In the spring of 1645 Charles was torn between two strategies. On the one hand he could relieve his port of Chester and try to join up with his Scottish supporters under Montrose to re-open the struggle for the north. On the other hand, it made good sense to attack the New Model Army while it was in its formative stages. Opinion within the royalist camp differed, with Rupert and Digby bitterly at odds. Characteristically, Charles tried to do both, and by dividing his forces left both armies outnumbered. Even so, Rupert would probably have avoided the worst effects had not Digby pushed the king into insisting that they attack a numerically superior New Model Army which was occupying a strong position outside the Leicestershire village of Naseby. The result, on 14 June 1645, was disaster. The parliamentary left flank was driven back by Rupert's cavalry, which promptly left the field of battle, but once more Cromwell's Eastern Association cavalry held firm and, having driven their royalist counterparts from the field, regrouped and destroyed the royalist infantry. The loss of his main army was bad enough for Charles, but worse was to come. When the royalist baggage-train was captured, the king's private correspondence came into parliamentarian hands. When it was published it revealed the extent of his duplicity. In the words of Derek Hirst:

1 The king's captured correspondence, published by parliament as The King's
   Cabinet Opened, revealed to the world his contempt for peace negotiations and his attempts to gain aid from all and sundry, including the
   Catholic Irish and the Pope; one leading Welsh royalist, Sir Trevor Williams,
5 promptly changed sides. Meanwhile Cromwell and others grew more confident that the hand of God was with them. *Authority and Conflict*, p. 257

The battle of Naseby was a turning-point, but it was not the end of the war. It destroyed the king's main field army, but there were other royalist forces, besides the countless local garrisons and fortified houses. Moreover, the king himself remained at large, and had no intention of giving up. However, there can be no doubt that the balance had swung decisively in favour of parliament. The New Model had gained in confidence and experience, and was able to follow up its victory by setting off in pursuit of the other main royalist army, which was commanded by Goring in Somerset. There Fairfax found local support in a population whom Goring had mistreated and suppressed, and in July, Goring was defeated at Langport. Two months later, on 10 September, Rupert surrendered the most important royalist stronghold in the south-west – the port of Bristol, in which the garrison was starving and the plague rife. It says much about the uncle whom he had faithfully served, that Charles never forgave this 'betrayal'.

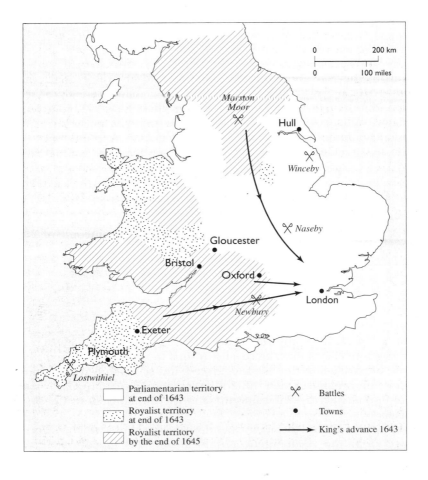

Yet the collapse of the royalist cause in England was not only the result of the successes of the New Model, but came equally from the resurgence of an older enemy – the forces of neutralism which reappeared in royalist areas with a strength born of war-weariness and desperation. The burdens of war had been enormous – not only in providing men and arms, but in supporting both main armies and local garrisons – and these burdens had fallen on a population already suffering from unemployment and the dislocation of trade. The problems are illustrated in a letter written to Viscount Fairfax (cousin of the parliamentarian general) from his agent at Alne, in Yorkshire, detailing the condition of his estates in May 1645:

I   I presently went to your tenants of your several manors to demand arrears. The answer of them all was ... that [with] the assessments paid to the armies, they were scarce able to pay anything. The tenants of Acaster Malbis ... had prepared a petition ... for relief, having sustained
5 above £2000 damage by the Scots... Skelton and Ampleforth, Gilling and Coulton lay so near Helmsley castle that during the time it was besieged, they were never without soldiers upon free billet ... who, besides their other provisions which they ate up, killed all their sheep.

By 1645 the whole country was impoverished and weary of war and for many the overriding concern was peace and survival. This growing demand for an end to the fighting was not directed towards helping one side rather than the other, although in specific areas neutralist groups did make alliances with the main protagonists when it suited their purpose. The aim of neutralism was peace, but in the circumstances of 1645, it worked to the benefit of parliament rather than the king.

4 The Resurgence of Neutralism, 1644–5

> **KEY ISSUE** How did the desire for peace affect the outcome of the war?

The first signs of the resurgence of neutralism came in the western counties held by the royalists, especially along the borders of Wales, and in South Wales itself. The defeats of 1644 had weakened the royalist grip in these areas, and the continuing existence of parliamentarian enclaves ensured heavy fighting and a heavy burden of rates. While claims that the royalist troops were less disciplined than those of parliament can be exaggerated, it was certainly true of some regiments, and the greater difficulties in keeping them regularly paid and supplied increased the amount of indiscriminate looting that took place.

For all of these reasons, it was the royalist cause which suffered more from the re-emergence of localism, and in particular the formation of Clubmen Associations. These were usually peasant associations, formed to protect property and supplies, which were often taken over and more fully organised by local gentry. They set out demands for a national peace and, meanwhile, sought to obtain an effective truce in

their own areas. There was no standard format. In Somerset, the initial impetus came from a group of royalist gentry in the winter of 1644–5, who sought to establish a local association that would work in conjunction with the king's forces. This was copied in Worcestershire, Herefordshire, Shropshire and Staffordshire where the gentry formed an association to impose local order and control the provisioning and maintenance of the royalist troops in the area. Again, this was not overtly anti-royalist, but sought to put local needs first and to regain control of the locality.

However, in January and March 1645, there were popular risings in these counties, which demanded the removal of all troops from the area. The response of the royalist generals was to make concessions to the gentry associations, and to crush the peasant risings. They could not, however, retain control of the situation, particularly after the destruction of the main royalist army at Naseby in June 1645. When the New Model Army advanced into Somerset they found the

Clubmen Associations of Wiltshire, Dorset and Somerset willing to co-operate in the effort to drive out the remaining royalists. This was not a matter of support for parliament, but a desire to regain control of the county, as their articles of Association illustrate:

1   The Desires and resolutions of the counties of Dorset and Wiltshire (Summer 1645)
    First: to maintain and defend the true reformed Protestant religion, and the inheritance of the crown.
5   Secondly: to join with and assist one another in the mutual defence of our liberties and properties, against all plunderers and against all other unlawful violence whatsoever ...

In this case the behaviour of Goring's royalist troops in plundering the area and the contrasting discipline of the New Model encouraged a tactical alliance between the Clubmen and the forces of parliament. Similarly, in the autumn of 1645 the Associations of South Wales were to declare for parliament, although a year later they were re-formed in an attempt to drive out the parliamentarian troops. The difference was that the latter retained the ability to respond, and the rising was crushed. The articles of the Sussex Clubmen of September 1645 were clearly directed against the parliamentary administration from which they had suffered, particularly in their complaints against unlicensed preachers and the 'want of Church government'. Again, however, the parliamentary cause suffered less because the administration had the power to deal with any disturbances.

The Clubmen Associations revealed the general unpopularity of the war, and raise doubts about the extent to which the population as a whole was ever committed to either cause. In practice, once the balance had tipped in favour of parliament, they did much to hasten the collapse of the royalist cause, but they were motivated less by a desire for parliamentary victory than by a wish to protect their own locality, or at most to see a speedy end to the war. As John Morrill put it,

1   There is overwhelming evidence that most of the Clubmen were neutrals ... This certainly did not preclude Associations from assisting either king or parliament in particular circumstances, but this need not imply a betrayal of their neutralism. A tactical alliance with Fairfax, for
5   example, helped the Devon and southern Somerset Clubmen to rid themselves of Goring, who represented a threat to provincial liberties far greater than that posed, in the short term, by the New Model. The Clubmen were not seeking to help parliament win the war. They were using parliamentary troops to clear their own counties of the most
10 potent immediate threat. [*Revolt of the Provinces*, p. 100]

Whatever their aims, however, the Clubmen movements worked to the benefit of parliament in weakening the royalist grip on its last remaining heartland. In the winter of 1645–6 the king remained at Oxford, seeking some strategy that might save him from surrender. Montrose and his Scottish supporters had been destroyed in September 1645, attempting to obey the king's command to come southward to his aid. Early in 1646 Charles offered to make Catholicism the official religion of Ireland if the Irish Confederates (the Catholic rebels) would come to his aid. Such desperate strategies achieved little as the New Model continued to mop up remaining royalist garrisons and strongholds. Finally, accepting the inevitable yet too proud to submit to a parliament, Charles left Oxford in April 1646 and gave himself into the custody of the Scots. Held at Newcastle, he listened to their proposals for Presbyterianism and received the Propositions of his English parliament for a diluted Presbyterianism in the Church and parliamentary control of the militia. He accepted neither, and, infuriated by his lack of response, the Scots gladly handed him over to the safe-keeping of parliament and withdrew from England (with a payment of £400,000 for their trouble). As Robert Baillie, one of the Scottish commissioners in London, predicted gloomily, 'that madman . . . will [take] down with him all his posterity, and monarchy'.

5 Conclusion; The Victory of Parliament

KEY ISSUE Why did Parliament win the first Civil War?

Parliament's victory resulted from a combination of factors whose role and importance in the final outcome needs to be carefully assessed. One way of doing this to consider which factors were conditional, creating an underlying probability of parliamentary victory, as opposed to those contingent factors which turned the probability into fact and influenced its shape and timing. These categories can also be used to assess the relative importance of different factors, and to show what combination of factors ultimately led to the victory of parliament.

It is clear that parliamentary control of the south-east and London provided superior resources, and that possession of the navy and the major ports of the kingdom enabled the parliament to stop the king from redressing the balance with supplies from abroad. Thus, one factor in parliament's success was its underlying superiority of resources. However, time was required to access these resources fully, and the initial advantage lay with the king. Hence the royalist failures of 1642–3 were also crucial. Determined resistance by pockets of parliamentary support, in particular the London trained bands after Edgehill and the ports of Hull, Plymouth and Gloucester in 1643, contributed to these. But the rivalries and differences among the royalist commanders were equally, if not more important. Newcastle's failure to march south in the summer of 1643 prevented an attack on London when parliamentarian fortunes were at their lowest ebb, and the continuing disputes between Prince Rupert and Lord Digby meant that strategic decisions were often influenced by personal considerations. Ultimately this failure of leadership must rest with the king, who had an authority denied to the parliamentary leaders. His hesitations and uncertainties, as well as the lack of judgement in choosing his advisers that he had shown all his life, contributed in no small measure to the royalist failure.

If royalist errors prevented an early royalist victory, they did not ensure parliamentary success. Without effective leadership, parliament would have been unable to use the breathing-space provided. Thus the skill of John Pym in balancing the opposing parties within the Commons, in persuading members to adopt new and unpopular methods of administration, and to accept a Scottish alliance was essential. As a result, the balance swung in favour of parliament, and it can be argued that the factors outlined so far created the probability, or likelihood, that the parliamentary forces would win the war, but that this was by no means certain. The failure of Essex in Cornwall showed how easily mistakes could be made, and resources drained. The final condition necessary for parliament's victory came with the military re-organisation of 1644–5, the emergence of leaders who sought victory as the pre-requisite of peace, and the establishment of the New Model Army. Thereafter, it is difficult to see that a royalist victory could have been possible.

If parliamentary victory was now inevitable at some time, it was by no means certain that it would be quick or complete. It was Charles's tactical error in fighting the battle of Naseby, and the re-emergence of neutralism, that brought royalist collapse within little more than a year. These contingent factors did much to speed up the process, but with resources already stretched and rivalries continuing, it is difficult to believe that the royalists were capable of matching the effectiveness of the New Model Army, or of reorganising themselves to become so. Had they been able to buy time it is perhaps possible that new divisions might have emerged in parliament, but the key factors in the ultimate outcome were already in place. By 1645 the combination of superior resources, superior leadership and superior military organisation had established the essential conditions for parliamentary victory.

Working on Chapter 4

Making notes on 'The Victory of Parliament'

The introduction to this chapter picks out the main factors that contributed to parliament's victory, while the account that follows explains parliament's success more fully through a broadly chronological structure. It is therefore best to approach note-making by using the structure of the chapter and breaking its sections down into sub-sections such as those suggested below.

Summary Diagram
Summary — The Victory of Parliament, 1643–6

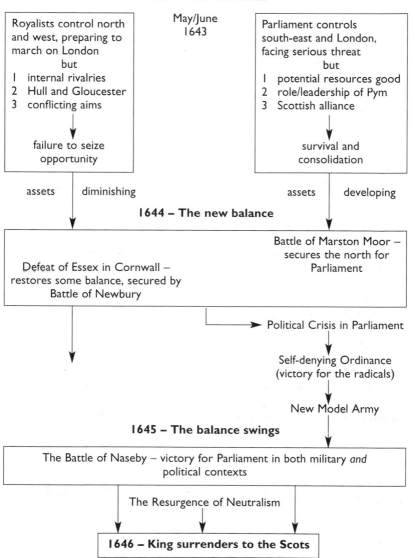

1643 – The two sides

| Royalists control north and west, preparing to march on London | May/June 1643 | Parliament controls south-east and London, facing serious threat |

Royalists control north and west, preparing to march on London
but
1 internal rivalries
2 Hull and Gloucester
3 conflicting aims

↓ failure to seize opportunity

Parliament controls south-east and London, facing serious threat
but
1 potential resources good
2 role/leadership of Pym
3 Scottish alliance

↓ survival and consolidation

assets | diminishing

assets | developing

1644 – The new balance

Defeat of Essex in Cornwall – restores some balance, secured by Battle of Newbury

Battle of Marston Moor – secures the north for Parliament

→ Political Crisis in Parliament

Self-denying Ordinance (victory for the radicals)

New Model Army

1645 – The balance swings

The Battle of Naseby – victory for Parliament in both military *and* political contexts

The Resurgence of Neutralism

1646 – King surrenders to the Scots

1. The failure of the Royalists
   a) leadership   b) internal divisions   c) limited resources
2. Parliamentary Assets
   a) military assets   b) financial resources   c) problems – accessing resources – internal divisions   d) leadership of Pym – organisation – maintaining unity – Scottish alliance
3. Parliamentary victory
   a) Pym's successors   b) Marston Moor; victory in the North
   c) political crisis and religious divisions   d) the Self-Denying Ordinance; the victory of the 'war' party   e) military reorganisation; the New Model Army   f) Naseby; the turning-point
4. The resurgence of Neutralism – the final phase and collapse of the Royalists

These notes should provide i) a brief chronological outline of the course of the war between 1643 and 1646, and ii) an explanation of the main reasons for, and key stages in the parliamentary victory. It would also be useful to summarise separately the role of key individuals such as the king, Pym, and the military leaders on both sides.

Answering essay questions on Chapter 4

Like the outbreak of war in Chapter 2, the victory of parliament is usually treated as an event, to be explained by identifying and examining a number of causal factors. Essay questions on the issue can take a wide variety of forms. At AS these may well be structured questions, such as:

1a) Describe the circumstances in 1644–5 that led to the formation of the New Model Army.
1b) Why did Parliament and its supporters emerge victorious in 1646?

while at A2 or in coursework units you may be faced with with more open questions, for example:

1. Why was parliament, rather than the king, victorious in the first Civil War, 1642–6?
2. To what extent was parliament's victory in 1646 inevitable?
3. 'A story of weak leadership and lost opportunities.' Does this accurately describe the reasons for royalist defeat in the first Civil War, 1642–6?
4. How far was Pym the architect of parliamentary victory in the first Civil War?
5. 'It was the New Model Army that gave victory to parliament.' How far do you agree with this judgement?

Although these questions appear to be phrased very differently, they are nevertheless all concerned with causation, and can be approached by defining and explaining a range of causal factors, as you have already learned to do. Question 1 sets out the issue in a straightforward fashion, while the other four questions all focus on particular factors which must be explained, and then assessed against other contributory elements. Question 2 places stress on the underlying trend and balance of forces, while 3, 4 and 5 emphasise more specific elements, which shaped and influenced the way in which those forces operated. In all cases, a good response demands that all of these factors be examined and their relative importance be compared and assessed.

One way of doing this, as demonstrated in the concluding section of the chapter, is to identify some factors as conditional and others as contingent. Historians often discuss causes as being long-term, or underlying, by which they mean that certain factors have built up over a period to create an underlying situation that makes a particular outcome possible or likely. Other causes are seen as short-term and less deep-rooted, influencing the timing, detail or precise form of that outcome. A more exact way of defining such factors is offered by the terms conditional and contingent. Conditional factors are those which create underlying conditions in which a particular event or outcome is likely. These are often long-term (such as the growth of religious discontent before the outbreak of war) but not always. Contingent factors, on the other hand, are those which trigger an event at a particular time, or dictate the precise nature of the outcome. These do tend to be short-term, and are often related to individual actions or specific events. To construct a good explanation of why parliament won the Civil War, you could apply these ideas to the factors outlined in Chapter 4, and then utilise them to plan and write one of the essays set out above.

1. Re-read the Conclusion of this chapter, plus your own notes and ideas, and construct a list of factors that contributed to the victory of parliament. Label each factor as conditional (creating the conditions which made parliamentary victory likely) or contingent (influencing when and how it occurred). For example, you could consider the failure of the royalists in 1643, the resources held by parliament, the roles of key individuals like Pym and Cromwell, the impact of the new Model Army, and the resurgence of neutralism. In each case, try to define any links between different factors, as well as the part that each one played. To do this, you may find it helpful to construct a spider diagram or flow chart.

2. Compare your ideas with those of others. To do this, you will have to explain exactly what part you think each factor played in the parliamentary victory, and you can then use these definitions to consider the relative importance of different factors by considering exactly how they worked together – for example, would parliament's underlying resources and assets have been important, had royalist mistakes and/or Pym's skill not given them time to be developed and realised?

4. In the light of these considerations and discussions, choose one of the essays listed to plan and write. Remember that the essay question will indicate the starting-point for your argument, but that you will need to consider all the factors that you have defined and to compare the role of any factor specified by the question against the influence of other factors in the whole combination.

5 The Emergence of the Radicals

POINTS TO CONSIDER

In 1646 the general expectation was that king and parliament would resolve their differences and negotiate a settlement. The logic of Charles's defeat was that he would now compromise, but this was not the case – Charles simply refused to accept this logic. Instead the king played for time, and waited for his enemies to fall out among themselves. The impact of the war and parliament's call to defend liberty had encouraged groups with radical ideas, who now believed that they had an interest in the settlement, and whose idea of 'liberty' was as incompatible with the attitudes of the majority in parliament as with the king. The result was a complex interaction of groups and interests, all seeking a settlement that reflected their hopes and aspirations, and all making that settlement more difficult to achieve. The complex nature of this process means that you will have to study the sequence of events carefully, to make sense of the different conflicts that emerged. In order to help you in this, the normal list of dates at the beginning of the chapter has been replaced with a table that traces the sequence of interaction between the competing interests, to explain the outbreak of the Second Civil War.

Introduction

By the end of 1646 it appeared that parliament would be able to achieve its objectives and establish a limited monarchy supported by a reformed Anglican Church. The king was defeated and the Scots had returned to Edinburgh, leaving the matter of a settlement in the hands of the English parliament. The soothing of widespread war-weariness by a return to normal government and a reduction of high war-time taxes seemed a real possibility. This would leave the governing class secure in its rights and privileges under the Crown. But this did not happen. Instead, the year that followed saw parliament faced with army mutiny and the collapse of negotiations resulting in the outbreak of a second civil war. In May 1647, the army defied orders to disband, in June it seized the king and began independent political negotiations. In July and August a three-cornered struggle for power between king, parliament and army developed. At the same time, the army leaders were engaged in their own struggle for control of the army itself, in the face of radical demands for the forcible dissolution of parliament and the establishment of a democratic republic. The year ended in political deadlock, which was broken by the king's instigation of a Scottish invasion and a Second Civil War in 1648. When

Date/event	ARMY	PARLIAMENT	KING
1646	Growing chorus of complaint from Presbyterian ministers and officers about radicalism in the Army, e.g. Thomas Edwardes in *Gangraena*	Sent revised version of *Nineteen Propositions* to king at Newcastle; included parliamentary control of militia and advisers, and Presbyterian Church Meanwhile turned to consideration of army and attack on radicals in London e.g. imprisonment of Leveller John Lilburne for slandering Speaker	Surrendered to Scots in the hope of gaining support, but refused to consider their terms, i.e. a Presbyterian Church Promised to consider parliament's proposals, and delayed his response
1647 January February		MPs voted to disband army except those who volunteered to fight in Ireland under new [Presbyterian] officers	King handed over to parliament: taken to Holdenby House, Northants
March	Soldiers petitioned via Fairfax for arrears of pay and indemnity	Responded by *Declaration of Dislike* and rejected petition	
April	Regiments elected Agents/Agitators to speak for them – some had links with Levellers, but demands still concerned with pay and indemnity	Appeals by Cromwell and other Independent MPs on behalf of army ignored by Presbyterians led by Holles and Stapleton. Disbandment fixed for June 1.	King finally rejected *Newcastle Propositions*

Date/event	ARMY	PARLIAMENT	KING
May	New, more radical Agitators elected. Signs of concern with wider settlement, especially religious liberty	27 May, order to army to disband issued	
	30 May, army announced refusal to disband and Agitators ordered Cornet Joyce to take king into army custody		
1647 June	3 June – Joyce visited Cromwell in London on way to take control of the king.		King Taken to Newmarket by Joyce and armed escort
	4 June – king seized		
	5 June – Regiments drew up Solemn Engagement [Cromwell and Ireton] and Fairfax agreed to set up Army Council		
	14 June – army issued Representation, declaring aims		
July	Cromwell and Ireton took lead in army plans – working on proposals for the king, resisting Leveller pressure for march on London to dissolve parliament	Army demands rejected by majority Presbyterians	

Date/event	ARMY	PARLIAMENT	KING
August	Fairfax ordered march to London to restore MPs. Army proposals presented to king on 2 Aug. Levellers accused officers [Grandees] of betrayal	Attack on parliament by London mob, orchestrated by Holles etc. and allies in City of London, drove out 60 Independent MPs including Speaker; they fled to army for protection Holles and other Presbyterian MPs left parliament to avoid army	Taken to Hampton Court; promised to consider army proposals
Sept./Oct	Levellers and some Agitators preparing alternative settlement *Case of the Army* and summary *Agreement of the People* and demanded debate in Army Council. Putney debates began in late October.		Rejected *Heads* but still discussing settlement.
November	Debates brought to an end by king's escape. Grandees refused to put *Agreement* to army at a single rendezvous		Escaped from Hampton Court to Isle of Wight, claiming fear of Leveller assassination. Nov.11
December	Leveller mutiny at Ware suppressed		Signed Engagement with Scots, initiating Second Civil War

In December, 1648 the king signed an *Engagement*, with the Scots initiating the Second Civil War that was over, the full importance of the new political and religious forces which had emerged in 1647 would be revealed.

The following chapter seeks to explain the emergence of these new forces during the course of 1647, and to assess their impact on events. It begins with an examination of the origins of radical groups and their ideas, and traces their development to the end of 1646. This provides the context in which the search for a settlement in 1647 revealed their existence and shaped their evolution. These events fall into three chronological sections leading up to the outbreak of the Second Civil War in early 1648. The first section demonstrates how parliament's initial actions in the spring of 1647 led to an army mutiny and considers the origins and nature of army resistance; the second traces the struggle for power between parliament and army in the summer of 1647 and explains the nature of divisions over the future settlement with the king; the third highlights radical development through explaining the Leveller challenge and its failure in the autumn of 1647. The chapter ends, therefore, with a reunited parliament and army facing the challenge of renewed civil war, and assesses how far the situation had changed as a result of the emergence of radicalism as a political and religious force.

1 The Origins of Radicalism

> **KEY ISSUES** Where did radical ideas come from? How did they develop in wartime conditions?

a) Roots and Origins

The origin of this radicalism was religious. The Protestant faith, emphasised individual belief, active commitment, and a personal relationship with God. Individual believers were encouraged to read and study the Bible, and were told that the rules of true faith were contained therein. Hence they were led to develop and believe in their own interpretations of a book that was part history, part myth and part poetry. Because some believed themselves to be chosen by God as his people they felt unable to remain within a Church which was only half-reformed by the Elizabethan Settlement of 1558–9. They were led, often by an inspirational preacher or minister, into the establishment of independent or separate congregations. Since these were illegal, and separation was, in itself, a subversive act, these congregations led a secretive and isolated existence; the effect of isolation and of continuing and enthusiastic internal debate was to encourage new and more unorthodox ideas to emerge. The Baptists, for example, had adopted the practice of adult, rather than infant baptism, as a commitment to church membership. Gifted members of such congregations were encouraged to debate with the minister (hence to question authority) and even to preach (officially the exclusive preserve of the educated, professional clergy). Thus traditional ideas of spiritual equality were given a new and practical expression. The General Baptists had even come to reject predestination itself, arguing that a loving God would open the gift of salvation to all who wished to receive it. In many ways the experience of the many forms of religious separatism undermined the concepts of social hierarchy and obedience to authority upon which seventeenth-century society and government rested and relied.

The attack on the authority of the bishops in 1641 led to the collapse of censorship. With access to a free press, radical arguments and ideas could be expressed publicly and could be openly debated. Lay preachers appeared in London. The outbreak of war heightened visionary ideas of a struggle between good and evil, and the victories of parliament's armies encouraged the belief that God approved their cause. Separatist churches operated with increasing confidence, and little could be done in wartime conditions to control their activities. In 1641 the London General Baptists held a joint conference, and in 1643 seven churches of the London Particular Baptists issued a joint *Confession of Faith*. In 1644 the first Independent, or Congregational, Church was founded in Hull, followed by another in Canterbury in 1645. By 1646, there were six such churches in Yorkshire alone. Most ominous of all for worried conservatives, by 1644 these separatists were demanding that any religious settlement should officially and permanently grant them the right to worship as they chose. While the Independent ministers in the Westminster Assembly of Divines asked only for a limited toleration, others such as Roger Williams (who later founded the American colony of Rhode Island) were denying that government should have any role in religion, and questioning the existence of any state Church, especially one supported by tithes (a compulsory local tax of one tenth of produce or income, to be paid to the parish clergy).

By 1644, therefore, religious radicalism had begun to challenge the very foundations of society and to develop new political ideas and demands. For the most part these came as a response to practical needs. Denial of religious freedom led to the formulation of arguments to justify it, and hence to theories about a wider range of rights and freedoms. In the same way, Presbyterian attacks on John Milton's ideas in favour of divorce led him to write and publish *The Areopagitica*, a passionately argued case for free speech and a free press. The number of separatists was always small, (a few hundred in 1644, probably no more than ten thousand at any time until the emergence of the Quakers in 1652) and the number of political radicals in their ranks even smaller, but the threat that they represented appeared enormous in conservative eyes. Moreover, by the end of 1646, two factors seemed to give real substance to their fears. The first was the emergence of a radical political movement in London in 1646, in the shape of the Leveller party; the second was the apparent strength of radical ideas within the New Model Army.

b) The Leveller Campaigns

> **KEY ISSUES** How did the Leveller movement develop? In what ways were the Levellers significant?

The Leveller party developed from the campaign for religious toleration which was under way in London by 1644. Its leading figures, John Lilburne, William Walwyn and Richard Overton, were all products of religious separatism. As an apprentice in London in the 1630s, Lilburne attended the sermons of Puritan preachers and was prosecuted by the High Commission in 1638 for smuggling and distributing banned religious tracts. When he was found guilty his punishment was to be whipped, pilloried and imprisoned. He used the public notoriety this treatment gained him both to attack the power of the bishops to imprison people and to assert his rights as a 'freeborn Englishman'. In 1641 he was released from prison by the Long Parliament and in 1642 he volunteered for parliament's forces. However, he left the army in 1644 in protest at the Solemn League and Covenant (the alliance with the Scots which included a promise to establish Presbyterianism in England). Returning to London, he seems to have joined a congregation of General Baptists, and was attracted to meetings of radicals at the Whalebone Tavern, where campaigns for religious toleration were beginning to be organised. There he made the acquaintance of the wealthy merchant William Walwyn, and the radical pamphleteer, Richard Overton. These three formed the core of a radical group arguing for complete freedom of belief and worship as a right for all.

By 1645 these radicals were well known for their views, and conservative enemies were eager to stop their activities. In July, Lilburne was accused of slandering the Speaker of the House of Commons, William Lenthall, and imprisoned on parliament's orders. His response was to publish a pamphlet *England's Birthright Justified* in which he protested at being imprisoned without proper trial, and accused the House of tyranny. He developed the argument into a demand for social and legal equality. By July 1646 the Levellers as a group were sufficiently notorious to merit a special section in Thomas Edwards' *Gangraena*, a bitter attack upon various radical groups which sought to alert parliament to the danger that they represented. Lilburne was accused by the Presbyterian William Prynne of slander against the House of Lords. Called by the Lords to answer the charges, he stood at the bar of the House, refused to remove his hat, and harangued the Lords for their injustice in thus summoning him.

He was once again imprisoned, but this led to a campaign by his wife and other Levellers for his release, in which Lilburne's experiences were used as the basis of demands for more wide-ranging political reform. Petitions, demonstrations and marches were organised in London, and pamphlets by Lilburne and others were published, setting out an increasingly comprehensive and coherent programme of political, legal and economic change. In a petition delivered to the Commons, entitled *A Remonstrance of Many Thousand Citizens* the Levellers claimed that the war had been waged for liberty, and that citizens should now be given their rights. The parliament was accused of being concerned only with its own interests. The argument drew together an attack on the monarchy, demands for political rights (including religious toleration) and a range of popular grievances over economic, social and legal inequality. It laid the basis for a wide-ranging programme of reform and a new form of government, based on a parliament elected by, and responsible to, the people as a whole.

c) A Radical Army?

> **KEY ISSUES** Was the Army a radical force? How did this influence the search for a settlement?

While parliament might ignore the Leveller petitions and demonstrations, they could not but be concerned by the evidence of religious radicalism in the ranks of the New Model Army. Not only did the soldiers preach, pray and debate among themselves (with and without the help of their chaplains and ministers) but complaints from many parts of the country showed that they encouraged and protected civilian separatists wherever they went. The first Congregational Church in England, at Dagger Lane in Hull, was established and encouraged by the Independent minister, Philip Nye with the help of the garrison preacher, John Canne. Nor was this malign influence limited to the lower ranks – Cromwell himself and many other officers were known to regard a man's religious beliefs as his own private affair, and to have protected those of unorthodox or radical views from punishment or persecution. In 1645 the moderate Presbyterian minister, Richard Baxter, had visited the army at its quarters near Naseby and been appalled by what he found.

1   We that lived quietly in Coventry did keep to our old principles and
    thought all others had done so too, except a few very inconsiderable
    persons ... we believed that the war was only to save the Parliament
    and Kingdom from papists and delinquents, and to remove the dividers,
5   that the King might again return to his Parliament; and that no changes
    might be made in religion, but by the laws which had his free consent
    ... And when the court news-book told the world of the swarms of
    Anabaptists in our armies, we thought it had been a mere lie, because

it was not so with us, nor in any of the garrison or county forces about
10 us. But when I came to the army among Cromwell's soldiers, I found a
new face of things which I never dreamt of: I heard them plotting, very
hot upon that which intimated [suggested] their intention to subvert
both Church and State. Independency and Anabaptristry were most
prevalent ... Abundance of the common troopers, and many of the offi-
15 cers, I found to be honest, sober, orthodox men, and others tractable,
ready to hear the truth, and of upright intentions; but a few proud, self-
conceited, hot-headed sectaries had got into the highest places, and
were Cromwell's chief favourites, and by their heat and activity bore
down the rest, or carried them along with them, and were the soul of
20 the army ... I found that many honest men of weak judgements and
little acquaintance with such matters, had been seduced into a disputing
vein, and made it too much of their religion to talk for this opinion and
for that; sometimes for State democracy and sometimes for Church
democracy.

It was hardly surprising that such an army should cause concern,
which grew as complaints multiplied throughout 1646. According to
Thomas Edwards,

1 The army that is so much spoken of upon all occasions in the news-
books, pulpits, conferences, to be Independent (though I conceive upon
good information, that upon a true muster of the whole ... there would
not be found above one in six of that way); yet of that army, called by
5 the sectaries, Independent, and of that part of it which truly is so, I do
not think there are 50 pure Independents, but more high-flown ...
made up and compounded of Anabaptism, Antinomianism [believing
that those whom God had saved were incapable of sin] Enthusiasm,
Arminianism [believing that salvation was open to all], Familism [believ-
10 ing that God existed within all]; all these errors and more too sometimes meeting in the same persons ...

His intemperate language and willingness to raise every possible
nightmare had its effect on MPs. With soldiers concerning themselves
in matters of 'church democracy and state democracy' in Baxter's
words, it is not surprising that conservatives feared the worst. That
such radicals constituted a small minority, even within the army, was
less important and less influential than the fact that they existed at all.
It was therefore all the more important, in the minds of many MPs,
that a settlement with the king should be concluded, which would
restore the traditional structures and controls provided by the partnership of monarchy and parliament.

2 The Parliamentary Search for Settlement

> **KEY ISSUES** What were the aims of the majority of MPs in
> 1646–7? Why did they handle the Army so badly?

a) The Concerns of Parliament

By the end of 1646, with the king effectively under house arrest at
Holdenby in Northants, and the Scots paid off to return to
Edinburgh, MPs were free to attend to the establishment of peace.
While most MPs assumed that Charles would have to come to some
agreement, however reluctantly, the old problem of trusting him to
maintain it remained a serious obstacle. Parliamentary control of the
armed forces and of the king's advisers would do much to overcome
this, always assuming that Charles would be prepared to listen to their
advice! An equally contentious area was the nature of the Church settlement. In 1645–6 the Westminster Assembly of Divines had finally
issued a *Directory of Worship*, which instituted a mild form of
Presbyterianism, and in some areas, such as London, this had been
partially established in practice. However, when these schemes were
put to the king in the form of the proposals presented to him at
Newcastle, Charles made it perfectly clear that they were unacceptable. As long as he remained in Scottish hands, his attitude created
the possibility that he might join with the Covenanters to renew the
war. Their insistence on rigid Presbyterianism in the Church was even
less palatable to him; but their willingness to restore his political
power might yet prove sufficiently attractive to persuade him to
accept their religious goals in the hope of overturning them later
when he had greater room for manoeuvre. Once he was in the hands
of the English parliament, however, this danger receded, and the parliamentary leaders felt able to wait upon developments with the king
while busying themselves with more immediate problems.

These revolved to a great extent around the instrument of their
success: the New Model Army. In the first place, the army was expensive and the population was increasingly resentful of heavy taxation.
The war-weariness of a nation which had borne unprecedented levels
of expenditure, as well as destruction and the dislocation of trade, was
a factor which parliament had to consider, especially as it might well
operate in favour of the king. Now that the threat of renewed war had
receded, it was natural that the remedy of disbanding the army should
be considered. In addition, the army's reputation for political and
religious radicalism horrified the majority of MPs. In 1644–5 the
needs of war had seen the more radical MPs able to dominate the
House of Commons, but the advent of peace had changed the situation. In order to make itself more fully representative of the political
nation, parliament had held by-elections in the seats occupied by roy-

alists. The hundred or so of these 'recruited' MPs elected in 1645 were mainly supporters of the war effort, but the further 135 elected in 1646 were largely concerned with the return of peace and 'normality'. This strengthened the conservative 'peace party' of the early war days. In this situation the peace leaders, Denzil Holles and Sir Philip Stapleton, had regained much of their earlier influence and they were eager to consolidate this and weaken the radicals by getting rid of their primary weapon, the army. It was therefore neither unreasonable nor surprising that they should seek both to solve parliament's financial problems and to rid themselves of an uncomfortable ally by proposing the disbandment of the army in early 1647.

b) The Army Mutiny

This proposal was enthusiastically received by MPs, who voted in favour in February 1647. Most regiments were to be disbanded, but a few were invited to volunteer for service in Ireland, where a campaign to deal with the rebels of 1641 was at last under way. These were to have new officers, and those who had previously been excepted from the *Self-Denying Ordinance* (Cromwell and others such as his son-in-law, Henry Ireton, who had been 'recruited' in 1645–6) were to return to parliamentary duty. On the face of it these were reasonable measures, but it did not escape the notice of the troops that the officers they would lose were all sympathisers with Independent or sectarian religious views, and that their replacements were more orthodox in outlook. More seriously, the disbandment made no allowance for payment of the soldiers' arrears of pay, nor gave them indemnity from prosecution for acts carried out during the war. These were issues of

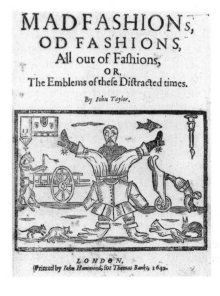

great concern to the rank and file. Many had not received adequate pay for months, and it has been estimated that by the end of the war, parliament's various armies were owed something in the region of £3 million. Indemnity was also a serious matter. Already by early 1647 there were reports of ex-troopers being hanged for theft as a result of requisitioning horses under orders during the war. Without legal protection from parliament, many of parliament's troops would be at risk of such prosecutions.

In March, therefore, the army petitioned their General, Sir Thomas Fairfax, to seek changes on their behalf. At this point the petitions were almost exclusively concerned with pay and indemnity rather than political or religious matters, and there is little doubt that concessions on these issues could have secured the peaceful disbandmant of many regiments. However, Holles had little sympathy for military concerns, and the death of the Earl of Essex in September 1646 had robbed him of expert military advice. He dismissed arguments that parliament could afford some payment of arrears, and persuaded the House of Commons to publish a *Declaration of Dislike* on 30 March, declaring the petitioners to be 'enemies of the state and disturbers of the public peace'. It was a serious misjudgement, and infuriated the soldiers, who had fought for the cause of parliament and considered themselves worthy of its gratitude rather than such condemnation. In April a number of cavalry regiments (always better educated than the infantry, many of whom were conscripted men) elected Agents or 'Agitators' to represent their views and these joined with the junior officers to voice the army's discontent. Again, there was little reference to religion at this point, but it is noticeable that a number of the representatives were Baptists, although this may only indicate that they were among the more articulate of the troops, having had experience of debate and public speaking in their religious meetings. Whether or not religious matters were a major cause of concern at first, they were to become increasingly important in the months that followed.

Despite appeals by Cromwell and other MPs who were sympathetic to the soldiers' claims, the conservatives pressed ahead, ordering the disbandment to take place on 1 June. On 31 May two regiments mutinied, and the crisis rapidly came to a head, despite concessions from parliament. The soldiers were now convinced that the conservative MPs intended to betray the cause for which they had fought, and would conclude an agreement with the king that would sacrifice their political and religious liberties. A meeting of the Agitators ordered Cornet Joyce to secure control of the king, probably in order to prevent any such agreement. On 3 June Joyce met Cromwell in London, and probably informed him of the army's intention. On 4 June Joyce removed the king from Holdenby House, and took him to the army's headquarters at Newmarket. On 5 June the regiments met in a general rendezvous and accepted the Solemn Engagement by which the army declared its refusal to disband until a just settlement which guaranteed the rights of 'freeborn Englishmen' was obtained. The Solemn Engagement also established a General Council of officers and agitators to co-ordinate the army's campaign. The same day Cromwell left London and rejoined the army, making public his support for its cause. Finally, on 14 June the army published its *Representation*, in which its political programme was outlined and its political intervention justified.

Written by Henry Ireton, who was to become the army's most influential political thinker, the *Representation* demanded a purge of corrupt MPs who were willing to betray parliament's cause, naming eleven conservatives including Holles and Stapleton. The present parliament was to be dissolved as soon as practicable, and future parliaments should be of fixed duration. The Church was to be reformed, and toleration granted to 'tender consciences' – those, like the Independents and Baptists, who believed that the state Church was not a 'true' church of believers, or objected to some of its practices, and preferred to worship in their own voluntary congregations. The document represented the emergence of the army as a political force, both in its radical demands, and in their justification. 'We are not', it declared, 'a mere mercenary army', but a body of volunteers who had responded to parliament's call to defend liberty. As such, the soldiers had a right to participate in establishing the settlement for which they had fought, and for which their comrades had died. Whatever settlement might emerge from this crisis, it was clear that it could no longer be concluded by king and parliament alone – a new and radical element had emerged onto the political scene.

c) The Politicisation of the Army

> **KEY ISSUE** What factors motivated the Army's intervention in the political settlement?

It is important to analyse how and why this political evolution of the army had occurred. There is no doubt that the misjudgements of parliamentary conservatives had been largely responsible for the first stirrings of resistance, and that many soldiers were, and remained, motivated first and foremost by material concerns such as pay and arrears. Historians of the army, from C.H. Firth to Mark Kishlansky and Austin Woolrych, have shown clearly that the New Model Army was not made up of political and religious visionaries, but contained many conscripted or mercenary troops for whom the military life was a profession rather than a crusade. Nevertheless, the speed with which political and religious demands were formulated, the coherence of the arguments and programme put forward and the determination and confidence displayed, by troopers and junior officers as well as the army leaders, suggests that the crisis arose from something more (and more deep-seated) than arrears and ingratitude.

The issue of how and why the army emerged as a political force has been fiercely debated among historians. Those who see 1648–9 as a year of revolution have stressed the emergence of radical ideas and the influence of the Levellers, while the 'revisionist' school of Kishlansky and others has emphasised the importance of material issues and the misjudgements of the conservatives. [The work of the historians named in this section has been summarised and evaluated in Barry Coward's *Stuart England*, pp. 138–40, 141–5.] It is clear that both elements played a part – what is at issue is their relative importance, and that must be carefully weighed against the evidence. On the one hand, there is no doubt that the behaviour of parliament was provocative, and that the material concerns of the soldiers were both widespread and real. There is little evidence of Leveller involvement until the crisis was well under way, in May 1647. In that month new Agitators were elected who included some troopers – Edward Sexby, William Allen and Captain White – who are known to have had Leveller connections. In the same month came the first clear expression of religious grievances and a demand for religious liberty. The army's *Engagement* of 5 June uses a typically Leveller reference to 'freeborn Englishmen', although it was actually written by the officer and MP, Henry Ireton. What is suggested by this evidence is that the crisis was created by conservative mistakes, and that the Levellers saw in the discontented soldiers potential allies for their cause.

However, if we consider why the conservatives made such misjudgements, the perspective is somewhat altered. It was the existence of radicalism in the army, at least in religion, which led conservatives to be anxious to dispose of it so quickly. The likelihood is that conservative fears were exaggerated, that radicals were few (as Baxter implied), but that they were not imaginary. Put together, the radical publications of the war years, including parliament's own appeals for resistance to tyranny, the spread of separatist congregations and the existence of religious radicals in the army do suggest that a new factor of some significance had emerged by 1646, which parliament's perceptions of a satisfactory settlement failed to take into account. The speed with which the army produced effective spokesmen, and the failure of parliament's concessions on pay and indemnity at the end of May indicate that for some, at least, the crisis reflected deeper concerns. If Leveller influence became important, it was because some common ideas, especially regarding religious freedom, had already taken root among the regiments. Moreover, what made the army so effective so quickly was the agreement achieved between officers and men, in which common concerns with political and religious issues played a vital role. While conservative mistakes undoubtedly dictated the shape and timing of the crisis, its origins lay in the impact and experience of war and the separate radical agenda that had developed among a small, but significant, minority of the population.

This argument is further strengthened by consideration of the way in which the army justified its political intervention. Ireton argued that the soldiers had fought for a cause in which they believed. They might not have been elected to represent the people in the matter of settlement, but they did represent the people of God, and God had publicly blessed their cause. His argument is clearly influenced by a belief, widespread in this period, in God's Providence as the deciding factor in the affairs of men. This belief, particularly strong among those of Puritan inclinations, emphasised God's direct control of events and asserted that God decided whether or not individuals should succeed in their endeavours. Thus the defeat of the king signified God's approval of parliament's cause, and the successes of the New Model Army meant that God had chosen and approved the army as the instrument of his Will. Hence the military had a special right, and duty, to participate in deciding what kind of settlement should emerge from the struggle.

It is inconceivable, therefore, that the behaviour of the army in the spring of 1647 can be understood without reference to its religion and the resulting interpretation of its wartime experience. The army was not an army of Saints, but there were Saints within it who believed in their duty to fight for God's cause, and who would never have stood by while parliament apparently betrayed it. Thus the conditions existing at the end of the war in 1646, which included the development of political and religious radicalism, made some kind of crisis among the supporters of parliament probable if not inevitable. The errors made by conservatives in response to these conditions ensured that the army would be united in this crisis, and that it would initiate a struggle in which parliament would be the loser.

3 Army, Parliament and King, June–November 1647

> **KEY ISSUES** How did the quarrel between army and parliament develop? How did the king seek to exploit these events?

a) The Aims of the Army

With the king safely in their hands and the soldiers united behind them, the army leaders now sought to establish an acceptable settlement. The key figures among the Grandees (the name increasingly applied to the senior army officers) were Oliver Cromwell and his son-in-law, Henry Ireton. Both of them were radical in religion, and therefore sympathetic to appeals for toleration. They were also members of the lesser gentry, sharing the belief in a hierarchical society and in the existing social and economic structures that was common to almost the entire ruling class. Of the two, Ireton was the better theorctician, but Cromwell approached the business of settlement with practical common sense, a desire for compromise and a sense of social justice which contributed a good deal to the proposals that emerged. In the 1630s he had sought to protect the rights of fen dwellers in East Anglia against the 'improvers' and their drainage schemes, not because he opposed the schemes, but because he believed that the dispossessed should be adequately compensated. Years later, as Lord Protector, he would claim that he was 'not wedded to forms' of government, and the same was true of his religious and social attitudes. His reputation for protecting religious radicals arose largely from the fact that his judgement of the soldiers who served him was based on their military merit, with little regard for their social origins or religious views. Hence his well-known praise of 'plain, russet-coated captains'. Equally, in defending an Anabaptist from persecution by the Presbyterian Major-General Crawford, he argued that a man's religious views should be a private matter – 'the State, in choosing men to serve them, takes no notice of their opinions'.

The settlement proposed by these men, with the help of the junior officer John Lambert, was a masterpiece of compromise. It was more generous to the king than parliament's *Newcastle Propositions*, offering the return of his legislative veto, control of the militia after ten years, and the restoration of bishops in the Church, albeit without coercive powers. Liberty of conscience would be granted to all but Catholics. Only five royalists were to be excepted from a general pardon. In addition, the proposals included provision for social and legal reform, parliamentary elections every two years, and a redistribution of parliamentary seats on the basis of taxation. Historians (particularly historians of the Levellers) have seen Leveller influence in these latter provisions, and this may well have been the case, but there is nothing in the proposals that did not accord comfortably with the attitudes and practice of Cromwell both before and after 1647. (For evaluation of these and other peace proposals presented to Charles, a comparative chart has been included as an Appendix at the end of this book).

Under the title of the *Heads of the Proposals* these ideas were presented to the king on 2 August. By now the crisis had moved on to divide parliament itself, and the army was approaching London. The move had been sparked off by conservatives in the city. Furious at the army's resistance to disbandment and its demand that Holles and ten other MPs should be impeached, the city merchants and clergy offered loans to pay for disbandment and the London militia to defend parliament. Dislike of religious radicalism, disorder and continuing expense provided a powerful motivation, and the increasingly royalist London mobs were encouraged to demonstrate for a settlement with the king. In July the mob invaded parliament itself, and 58 MPs, including the Speakers of both Houses, fled to the army for safety. With this stamp of authority and legitimacy, Fairfax began a slow march on London, the city militia melted away, and the 11 MPs named by the army for impeachment fled. On 4 August the army entered London unopposed.

b) Presbyterians and Independents: the politics of settlement

> **KEY ISSUES** What underlying issues created the divisions within parliament and army? Why do historians use religious labels to define political quarrels?

This parliamentary crisis of July undermines any assumptions of a simple division between army and parliament, suggesting rather that parliament itself was divided over the nature of the settlement that was desired. Throughout the spring the initiative had been held by the conservative group gathered around Denzil Holles and the Committee for Disbandment who met at Derby House. The majority of MPs were content to support this group, but there were some who were more sympathetic to the army's aspirations, and who shared their religious views and distrust of the king. Because the conservatives broadly supported parliament's Presbyterian scheme of church reform, and the opposing minority were sympathetic to a measure of religious toleration, they have been labelled political Presbyterians and Independents, but such labels disguise as much as they reveal. In the first place, the groups did not really conform to these religious divisions. Many conservatives, such as Holles, could happily accept bishops in the Church, provided their power was reduced and parliament's supremacy asserted. In contrast, some religious Presbyterians, such as Zouch Tate and Isaac Penington, aligned themselves with the army. Secondly, it is erroneous to visualise clear-cut groups at all. Most MPs behaved as individuals, attempting to pick their way through a confused and confusing clash of ideas and personalities, to find a settlement for problems with which parliaments had never previously had to grapple. However, there were two core groups who shared beliefs and personal links. One centred on Holles, Essex and Stapleton, and the other on Vane, St.John, Haselrig, Cromwell and Lord Saye and Sele. They corresponded to some degree with the old 'peace' and 'war' parties, and each represented wider vision of settlement and how it was to be achieved. At different times and in different situations, the majority of uncommitted MPs accepted the lead of one or other group, as seemed appropriate.

For the Holles group, the restoration of order took priority – hence they supported 'Presbyterianism' because it seemed to offer the best prospect of an effective state Church which could fulfil its traditional role of maintaining social and political authority over the people. They regarded the king as the lynch-pin of order, and were willing to make significant concessions in order to restore him to his place. Hence the term 'conservative' seems most appropriate to describe them. We cannot, however, use the neatly opposed 'radical', let alone 'revolutionary', to describe the other party. Its members' attitudes were characterised by a deeper suspicion of the king and a greater determination to achieve guarantees of political and religious rights, rather than by an entirely different concept of what a settlement should be. If there was any religious characteristic common to the group, it tended to be a concern with religious, or spiritual matters, rather than a particular form of religion or membership of any denomination. Hence a church which could uphold social cohesion was essential, but no more so than 'liberty for tender consciences' within or alongside it. It could be said that the main difference between the two groups lay in their sense of priorities rather than in any clash of fundamental political vision.

In this situation, the army mutinies consolidated conservative support but posed a problem for its allies. Whilst sympathising with the soldiers' aspirations, they also believed in the rights and authority of parliament. In the end, Cromwell and other officers placed themselves at the head of the army revolt in order to maintain its unity and to exercise a restraining influence. Without a united army, their opportunity to influence the settlement would rest on their weak position as a parliamentary minority. In July, however, it was the conservative mobs in London who posed the threat to both order and the rights of parliament. Hence many uncommitted MPs joined those who took refuge with the army, and gave a legitimate reason for Fairfax's march on the city. What the divisions in parliament in the summer of 1647 most clearly indicate is the fluidity of the situation at this point. Its future development would depend very much on the nature of any agreement that the army leaders hoped to negotiate with the king.

c) The Attitude of the King

KEY ISSUE How did Charles view the situation?

Such hopes were now to be disappointed by the king himself. Charles had watched his enemies fall out, and had drawn the erroneous but appealing conclusion that he could use their differences for his own ends. This was an understandable response, especially given that the *Heads* were a significant improvement on parliament's earlier proposals. Moreover, there were genuine difficulties for Charles. Because he held authoritarian views and was wedded to a belief in his divine right, he would be reluctant to surrender control of religious belief to the extent that was suggested, let alone to give up control of the militia. Derek Hirst [*Authority and Conflict*, p. 277] has suggested that he would have found it hard to abandon his friends (the five excepted royalists), although Charles treatment of those, such as Prince Rupert, who had served him in war indicates that his conscience could be somewhat elastic in such matters. Most important, however, Charles did not believe that he needed to come to terms at this time. The major miscalculation of all those who sought to achieve a settlement with Charles was to assume that he would accept his military defeat as final. For Cromwell and the army, it was God's verdict on the conflict, but for Charles it was a temporary setback in his struggle to defeat a rebellion. He was the king, and there could be no settlement without him. He had other kingdoms – Scotland and Ireland – on whom he might legitimately call. If his enemies were falling out among themselves, he could afford to wait until one or other of them came round to his way of thinking. He therefore delayed his answer to the army's proposals and awaited parliament's reaction. Disappointing as this may have been for the army leaders, they had little time to dwell on it, since they were already engaged in a separate struggle for control of the army itself.

4 The Leveller Challenge, July–November 1647

a) Ideas and Influence

> **KEY ISSUE** What were the Levellers seeking to achieve through the army?

By early June 1647 it was clear that the Leveller movement had established at least a foothold within the army. Parliament's rejection of their plans had encouraged the Leveller leaders to look for alternative sources of support, and the discontents of the army rank and file provided fertile ground for their arguments. The army General Council provided a platform for Leveller demands and, although John Lilburne remained in prison throughout the summer of 1647, he was able to exercise an influence through Agitators like Edward Sexby and civilian contacts like John Wildman, a London Leveller who played a significant part in drafting the Agitators' declarations and claims. Leveller leaders wanted the dissolution of the Long Parliament and a new Assembly, elected on a wide franchise, and looked to the army to carry out the task. The Grandees' refusal, and their march on London to restore parliament's independence frustrated the radicals, and the continuing negotiations with the king provoked suspicions of a deal which would leave the Levellers isolated.

In an attempt to regain the initiative and refocus the army's efforts, Wildman issued a new political declaration, *The Case of the Army Truly Stated* in October. The document summarised the soldiers' grievances and wove them into a wider case for political reform based on a genu-inely representative parliament While it did not necessarily call for the removal of the king, power was deemed to be derived from the people, and their elected representatives were clearly regarded as being superior to any monarch. In order to exercise control of their representatives, the people were to have new elections every two years, and parliamentary seats were to be based on population. This clearly implied something akin to manhood suffrage. Government was to be further limited by certain fundamental laws, which guaran-teed political rights and liberties, including religious toleration.

The Case of the Army did not constitute a clear and coherent set of constitutional laws, but it did advance revolutionary and effectively democratic theories of government. Re-drafted into the *Agreement of the People* for debate in the army council, it drew on a number of sources. Parliament's own arguments about the 'ancient and funda-mental' constitution, the imposition of the 'Norman yoke' of monar-chy and the rule of law formed a base. But where parliament had claimed authority for itself to resist tyranny as a 'lesser magistrate', the Levellers had gone directly to the source of power, the people. The revolutionary step that they had taken in arguing that all people were capable of exercising political rights, owed much to the experience of the separatist churches, where spiritual equality and rights of debate had extended beyond the governing class. Most significant, where other churches had demanded these rights and freedoms for God's people, as privileges for the Saints, the Levellers accepted the General Baptist claim of salvation for all. Thus, if all were capable of salvation because God had given them the capacity to accept faith through human reason, then all were capable of exercising that reason in human affairs. Religious belief and experience had led them to a basic theory of human rights.

Extracts from the *Agreement of the People*

1   Having by our late labours and hazards shown at how high a rate we value our just freedom, and God having so far owned our cause as to deliver the enemies thereof into our hands, we do now hold ourselves bound in mutual duty to each other to take the best care we can for 5   the future ... Since, therefore, our former oppressions and scarce-yet-ended troubles have been occasioned, either by lack of frequent parlia-ments, or by rendering those meetings ineffectual, we are fully agreed and resolved to provide that hereafter our representatives be neither left to an uncertainty for the time nor made useless to the ends for 10 which they are called. In order whereunto we declare:
    That the people of England, being at this day very unequally distrib-uted by Counties, Cities and Boroughs for the election of their deputies in Parliament, ought to be more indifferently proportioned according to the number of the inhabitants ...
15   That to prevent the many inconveniences apparently arising from the

long continuance of the same persons in authority, this present
Parliament be dissolved upon the last day of September ... 1648.
    That the people do choose themselves a Parliament once in two
years ...
20   That the power of this and all future Representatives of this Nation
is inferior only to those who choose them, and doth extend ... to whatsoever is not expressly or impliedly reserved by the represented to
themselves: Which are as followeth,
    1 That matters of religion and the ways of God's worship are not at
25 all entrusted by us to any human power, because therein we cannot
remit or exceed title of what our consciences dictate to be the mind of
God without wilful sin: nevertheless, the public way of instructing the
nation (so it be not compulsive) is referred to their discretion.
    2 That the matter of impresting and constraining any of us to serve
30 in the wars is against our freedom; and therefore we do not allow it ...
    4 That in all laws made or to be made, every person may be bound
alike ...
    5 That as the laws ought to be equal, so they must be good, and not
evidently destructive to the safety and well-being of the people ...
35   These things we declare to be our native rights ...

b) Resistance and Failure

KEY ISSUE Why did the Levellers fail?

The Grandees were repelled by such revolutionary ideas. However,
they had little choice but to allow the debate. In late October and
early November the Army Council met in Putney Church, where
Agitators and some officers spoke in favour of the *Agreement*, while
Ireton led the challenge against it. The records of the debate are
incomplete, but it is clear that it came to revolve mainly around the
issue of the franchise, with Ireton arguing strongly in favour of the
representation of property and interests rather than people.
Cromwell's role was to contain the hostility of the debate, and seek
above all to protect the unity of the army. It is difficult to know what
the outcome would have been. Certain of Ireton's criticisms were
later accepted by the Levellers when they reduced the right to vote to
all 'free' men, removing the rights of servants, wage labourers and
paupers, but the argument did appear to be going the Levellers' way
when the whole procedure was brought to an abrupt end. On 11
November the king escaped from army custody, and made his way to
Carisbrooke Castle on the Isle of Wight.
    The king's escape was undoubtedly timely from the point of view
of the Grandees. Raising the possibility of renewed war, and a need to
restore military discipline. An attempt by the Levellers and Agitators
to have the army drawn up in a general rendezvous (where they

hoped to offer it the *Agreement*) was defeated by Cromwell, who called three separate rendezvous to gather the troops together. The first, held at Corkbush Field near Ware in Hertfordshire, saw an abortive mutiny led by the regiment of Colonel Robert Lilburne, which was quickly suppressed. Three troopers were arrested, and one shot – an indication of how limited and short-lived the mutiny was. The Levellers vented their fury in attacks upon the Grandees, but their position was weak. With the threat of a second civil war, they could hardly justify attacking the generals upon whose efforts the safety of parliament and the cause depended. By the time the war was over, the political scene had changed. Although the Grandees concluded a brief alliance with the Levellers in the autumn of 1648, they were again outmanoeuvred. A council of officers rejected a second version of the *Agreement* in December, and offered its own revised draft to parliament, where it was simply laid aside. In 1649 the king was executed, and the monarchy abolished without any reference to Leveller ideas. Later attempts to subvert the army in 1649 led to the crushing of a Leveller mutiny at Burford, and the disintegration of the movement. Although it was unclear in 1647, the defeat of the Levellers at Putney had meant the effective end of Leveller influence.

c) The Significance of the Levellers

What, then was the significance of the Leveller intervention in 1647? Despite the claims of the Leveller leaders, and of sympathetic historians, it is unlikely that they ever enjoyed widespread support. As a political party they built up a membership of several hundred in London, and were capable of organising demonstrations involving several thousands. They undoubtedly had some influence in the army, and were able to pressurise the Grandees. The king's escape eased Cromwell's difficulties in this area, allowing him to end the debates and restore military discipline. Some historians of the Levellers have even suggested that he organised the escape himself, for this very purpose, although there is only circumstantial evidence to support such a claim. Nevertheless, the ease with which discipline was restored and the Levellers outflanked suggests that their support was always limited, and dependent upon the particular circumstances of 1647. Outside London, they made little impact. It was the concentration of Leveller support in the political capital, combined with the coincidental divisions of parliament and army, that gave the party its influence at this time.

Nevertheless, the Levellers do have significance for the ideas that they developed and made public. Among the dozens of Leveller pamphlets published between 1646 and 1649, it is easy to point to weaknesses and inconsistencies. Leveller ideas were being developed partly as a vision of the future inspired by an unprecedented upheaval in society, partly as a political programme for immediate adoption, and partly as a propaganda campaign in a bitter power struggle. In these circumstances it is not surprising that their ideas and plans lacked a measure of coherence. Therefore, what is significant is not the fact that some ideas were impractical, nor that some changed or were abandoned, but that in the context of the seventeenth century they were formulated at all. Drawing upon widely accepted beliefs, religious enthusiasm and personal experience, they enunciated theories of democratic government and personal rights and freedoms which would never entirely disappear. The fact of their existence is evidence of the revolutionary nature of events in this period, even if it was a revolution conducted by a minority, and doomed to failure.

5 Conclusion; The Emergence of the Radicals

> **KEY ISSUE** How did the emergence of radical groups affect the search for a settlement between king and parliament?

The emergence and evolution of political and religious radicalism in 1646–7 was clearly not the sole reason for the failure to find a settlement after the First Civil War. That failure owed as much to the inflexible demands made by parliament and probably even more to the attitude and beliefs of the king. However, the development of new demands within the army did introduce new complexities, and did encourage Charles's hopes by dividing his enemies. Yet it is doubtful whether this had great significance in the outcome of events. The actions and attitudes that Charles had taken up since succeeding to the throne in 1625 all point to an inflexibility which would have led him to reject any settlement that parliament could have accepted, with or without divisions in the parliamentary ranks. Nor were those divisions serious enough to afford him a real prospect of reversing the military outcome of the war. The speed and effectiveness with which parliament and army reunited in 1648 meant that by late summer the king was again facing defeat.

This did not, however, mean that the differences between the aims and aspirations of the radicals in the army and the conservatives in parliament were short-lived or insignificant. The emergence of radicalism reflected important forces in English society, which had been developing and evolving since the reign of Elizabeth. While it is true that radical ideas influenced only a small minority of the population, and had been able to spread only because of the conditions and impact of civil war, they were, nevertheless, a logical outcome of a century of religious development in England. Once a minority had begun to challenge the authority of the Church and to question the role of the state in religion, issues were raised which could not simply be ignored. The attempt to do so in early 1647 had sparked off the very crisis that the conservatives had sought to avoid. The political and social aspirations of the Levellers could be contained with relative ease, because seventeenth-century England lacked the economic and social structure as well as the communications which would allow them to establish widespread support. Religious enthusiasm, however, was a more dangerous force, since it cut across class barriers. Thus the events of 1647 created a new political element in a united army, which claimed a role in the shaping of government and justified it by the will of God. They were capable of genuinely revolutionary solutions to the problems of settlement when the search was renewed in the autumn of 1648.

Summary Diagram
Summary – The Emergence of the Radicals

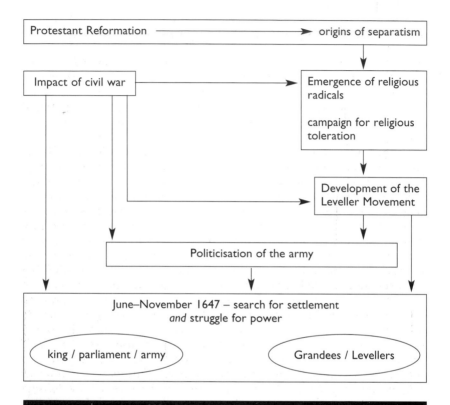

Making notes on Chapter 5

The structure of the chapter is clearly indicated by the headings included, and these will provide an overall structure for note-making. In order to maintain a clear sense of sequence and the interaction of groups and events. You may find it useful to construct a flow chart to summarise the development of the conflicts. This framework will make it easier for you to handle the detail required in your linear notes. As in previous chapters, you will find it useful to devise sub-headings for these, based on the key points within each section. For example, the section on the Origins of Radicalism could be sub-divided into:

1. The nature of Protestant ideas
2. The development of separatism
3. The effects of crisis, 1641–4
4. The Levellers and their ideas
5. The New Model Army.

This model should be followed for the other sections, with sub-sections being devised as appropriate.

Answering essay questions on Chapter 5

There are a number of possible questions which can be answered from Chapter 5. For example, the central theme of why Radical groups emerged draws on both the events of the Civil War period and the earlier development of Protestant and Puritan beliefs. It can be argued that the nature of Protestantism provided the basic conditional factors leading to separatism and potentially radical ideas, while the break-down of censorship, the upheaval of the Civil War and the New Model Army enabled radicalism to emerge as a powerful force at this time. Similar questions can be asked about the rise, and failure, of the Levellers. The chapter also addresses questions about the failure to negotiate a settlement and the role of radical forces in this failure as compared to the mistakes of the parliamentarians and the intransigence of the king. These may stand alone, or be utilised in other, more wide-ranging essays – such as why parliament won the war and lost the peace. In addition, of course, this material is essential for explaining the execution of the king – which is discussed in the next chapter.

The questions below offer possible essays, for both AS and A2 papers, based on the concept of causal factors which you have already addressed. The best causal essays, however, aim to *evaluate* the role of different factors, perhaps by considering their *relative importance*. It is not enough simply to assert the importance of one or other factor – it has to be argued on the basis of evidence. One way of doing as suggested on pp. 97–8 is by looking at the relative roles of conditional and contingent factors. Another is by considering whether the absence of a particular factor would have changed the outcome – in other words, whether that particular factor was necessary for the event to take place. For example, the origins of religious radicalism lay in Protestant beliefs and the supremacy of the Bible. However, until the War, which brought about the collapse of censorship and social control in 1640–1, separatist groups were small, isolated and often short-lived. Thus the wartime freedom can be seen as necessary for the development of radicalism. The spread of separatism was encouraged by the existence and mobility of the New Model Army, but it is likely that separatism would have developed a significant base even without this. Thus it can be said that Protestantism and the breakdown of controls were sufficient to explain the emergence of radicalism, which was merely accelerated by the activities of the New Model Army.

Plan an outline response to each of the essay questions listed below, using the idea of necessary factors and sufficient causes to explain their relative importance. (This could usefully be done in discussion with a group or partner).

1. Why did political and religious radicalism develop during the Civil War?
2. Why did parliament fail to establish an effective settlement after the First Civil War?
3. Why did the Levellers fail?
4. How far was the failure to find a settlement after the First Civil War the result of the attitudes and actions of Charles I?
5. Why did parliament win the war and lose the peace?

Source-based questions on Chapter 5

Radical ideas and actions offer a rich source of documents, and are likely to figure in source-based examinations on this period. When dealing with such documents, it is important to read them slowly – perhaps by reading aloud – and to break them down into points and paragraphs rather than trying to deal with the document as a whole. You will also need actively to engage your background knowledge, to try to identify the ideas, actions and attitudes that are referred to. Exercise 1, below, is intended to help you analyse and interpret the documents in Chapter 5. Exercise 2 introduces a higher level task, using evidence to test hypotheses and develop arguments.

Exercise 1 – Source Analysis

1. Read Baxter's description of the Army on p. 106. What does the source reveal about the ideas and attitudes of the soldiers? [comprehension/interpretation] *5 marks.*
2. In what ways is Baxter's evidence supported by Thomas Edwards on p. 107? [interpretation/cross-reference] *5 marks*
3. How far do you consider these sources to be reliable? [evaluation, cross-reference] *5 marks*
4. What do you believe to be the intended message of the illustration on p. 109? [interpretation] *3 marks*
5. How does this help to explain the attitude of Baxter and Edwardes? [cross-reference] *3 marks*
6. Read the extracts from the *Agreement of the People* on p. 118–19. Summarise the main features of the proposed constitution. [comprehension] *5 marks*
7. What does the *Agreement of the People* reveal about Leveller aims and beliefs? [interpretation] *8 marks*
8. In what ways do the contents of the *Agreement* and the picture of the Army Council on p. 120 help to explain why the Levellers failed? [interpretation in context, cross-referencing to draw conclusions] *6 marks*

Exercise 2 – Testing Hypotheses

A hypothesis is an idea or theory, in this case about historical events and issues. Historical enquiry involves collecting information in order to define key issues and develop a series of hypotheses about them, before conducting further research to test, refine and develop them into an overall 'thesis' – an interpretation of the past. This process can be reduced to a manageable task in order to practise the skills involved, in two ways. The first is to offer an hypothesis for testing against evidence from sources, or in a more sophisticated version, to offer two competing hypotheses to be tested, adjusted and reconciled into an overall judgement. The second involves the same process in the form of an essay, where a judgement is offered and tested against knowledge of events. Hence these techniques also offer a more general approach to planning essays, as an alternative to the 'causal factor' method that you have previously addressed.

1. Using the sources analysed in exercise 1, collect evidence to support and challenge the hypothesis that: 'The Levellers failed because their plans were too radical for the society that they lived in'.
2. Repeat the process to test the statement that: 'The Levellers failed because they could not win control of the army'.
3. In the light of your testing, adjust and synthesise the two statements into an explanation of the failure of the Levellers.

These steps will enable you to use hypothesis testing as a way of developing your own judgements. However, you will also meet essay questions that require you to evaluate a judgement such as question 4 on p.125. These often begin with 'To what extent' or 'How far', or offer a quote such questions, by arguing for and against statement and ask if you agree. This technique of hypothesis testing is an ideal way of approaching/the claim in the question, before coming to a balanced judgement in the conclusion.

6 The Second Civil War and the Execution of the King

POINTS TO CONSIDER

The execution of Charles I was the climax of a decade of upheaval, a shocking event that echoed across Europe. It was also the unexpected outcome of the attempt to find a settlement after the Civil War, not contemplated by any until the middle of 1648 at the earliest. It can therefore be presented as the result of short-term factors. Chapter 6 begins by examining the process of how it came about, as a prelude to explaining why. When you have read the first section, you need to make accurate notes about the events leading up to the execution, and explore the ideas that motivated such revolutionary action. You should do this before working on the rest of the chapter.

If the term 'revolutionary action' is justified – if there was a revolution in January 1649 – it seems unlikely that it can be explained entirely by short-term factors. The second part of the chapter therefore explores the roots of the event, to set the short-term factors into a wider context, and by analysing and summarising this material, you will be able to develop your own view of both its causes and its significance.

DATE LIST

1648	**January**	In response to the king's *Engagement* with the Scots, Parliament voted 'No Further Addresses' to the king.
	March–June	Royalist risings spread across south-eastern England, backed by scattered outbreaks in the north, Cornwall and Wales. South-east brought under control by Fairfax, except for Colchester, besieged from June 14.
	April	Army prayer-meeting at Windsor called for justice against Charles, the 'man of blood'.
	June	11 MPs previously expelled from the Commons by the Army re-took their seats. House rescinded the vote of 'No Further Addresses'.
	July	Welsh risings ended with surrender of Pembroke Castle to Cromwell. Scots entered England, harried by Lambert on march south.
	August	Scots defeated by Cromwell and the New Model Army at Preston [17th–19th]. Colchester surrendered to Fairfax, Aug. 28

September	Parliamentary commissioners renewed negotiations with the king on the basis of 'Four Bills'.
November	Army Remonstrance called for trial of the king.
December	On 5 Dec. Parliament voted for further negotiations and return of the king to London, on 6 Dec. Col Pride purged parliament.
1649 January	On 1 Jan. the 'Rump' of MPs agreed to set up a High Court to try the king; 6 Jan. Court was established.
20 January	Trial began, 30 Jan. Charles I beheaded at Whitehall.
March	Monarchy and House of Lords abolished, England declared to be a Commonwealth.

1 The Execution of the King, 1648–9

> **KEY ISSUE** How can such a shocking and unexpected event be explained?

Charles I was executed on 30 January, 1649. He died a martyr at the hands of the army and a minority of MPs, against the will of the English people. In order to make this possible, parliament had been purged in early December 1648, with approximately 186 MPs forcibly excluded and another 45 imprisoned. A further 169 chose to be absent from the House until the execution had been carried out, although over 80 resumed attendance during the month of February 1649 and thus participated in the formal abolition of the monarchy and House of Lords in March. Only 71 of approximately 500 members of the Commons actively participated in the king's trial and execution, and of the 135 men named to be judges in the special High Court on 1 January, over half, including Sir Thomas Fairfax, refused to serve.

It is clear, therefore, that this was not the outcome sought by the majority of those who had fought against the king – yet it was the outcome of the Civil Wars. Even if these events are defined as the acts of a minority, as the description above suggests, it is necessary to explain why even a minority were prepared to bring an anointed monarch, God's representative on earth, to public trial and execution, and how they were in a position to do so. If we also consider why the majority did not share this determination, we may be able to highlight the importance of particular factors, and perhaps to understand why the 'revolution' thus enacted proved ultimately to be unsuccessful.

The following chapter approaches these issues in two ways. The first section traces the main events of 1648–9 to demonstrate how and why a minority of MPs, backed by the power of the army, brought the king to trial and execution. This is followed by a study guide, suggesting how you might construct effective notes on this material, and using source-based questions to explore some ideas more fully. The second section then focusses on the key question of why Charles was executed in 1649, and draws on both the material and the methodology outlined in earlier chapters to construct a response. This is intended to demonstrate the use of the methodological tools that have been introduced and developed through the different study guides, and to enable you to develop your own responses to a number of possible essay questions on this topic.

a) The Second Civil War

> **KEY ISSUE** In what ways was the Second Civil War significant?

Militarily, the Second Civil War was of little significance. The 'rebel' forces fell into three main groups with little in common other than a dislike of the existing central authority and its policies. Among ex-parliamentarians as well as royalists there was a desire for a return to normal and familiar forms of government and resentment of the county committees and their ordinances. In Canterbury in December 1647, the parliamentary ordinance against the celebration of Christmas led to riots. When parliament, reacting to the king's *Engagement* with the Scots, passed a vote of *No Further Addresses* (to the king) in January 1648, outraged gentry organised local petitions calling for a treaty with the king and the disbandment of the army. In the spring of 1648 these local resentments led to disturbances in London and Norwich and outright rebellion in Kent, Essex, South Wales and in sections of the navy. The parliamentarian supporters who led these outbreaks were seeking to influence the decisions of parliament rather than to restore the king on his own terms, and the half-heartedness of their campaigns meant that they were quickly dealt with once the army stirred itself in April. More genuinely royalist were the cavalier risings in Cornwall, Yorkshire and Wales, but the majority of ex-royalists were unwilling or unable to react in support. Only in Wales and in Essex, where the royalists capitalised on wider discontent to seize control of Colchester, did lasting campaigns result. Colchester was besieged by Fairfax for several months, while Cromwell led a detachment of the New Model Army into Wales.

The third element of the king's support, the Scottish army, entered England in July. Despite the Engagement, the Scots had been slow to raise forces, and were further hampered by quarrels between the nobility and the Kirk (Presbyterian Church, whose ministers had great influence in the Scottish Lowlands). Dogged by bad weather in England, the Scottish army struggled into Lancashire where they were harried and delayed by Colonel John Lambert's Yorkshire troops. In August, Cromwell, having completed his task of suppressing the South Wales rebels, turned north to catch the Scots at Preston on 17

August. In two days he had destroyed their much larger force, bringing any significant royalist threat to an end. Although the siege of Colchester lasted another 10 days, and mopping up operations in Yorkshire occupied Cromwell himself until early December, the war had effectively finished before August was ended.

In political terms, however, the war was hugely important. On the one hand, the conservative case for a compromise peace was enormously strengthened, while on the other, the army became adamantly opposed to any such treaty. Although the rebellions had been ill-coordinated and ineffective, the widespread unrest revealed popular dislike of parliament's attempts to reform religion and manners and the resentment of the local elites against its control of local government. The title of John Morrill's study of localism in the Civil Wars, *The Revolt of the Provinces*, was inspired by the Second Civil War. The House of Commons responded by rescinding its vote of *No Addresses*, allowing negotiations to be re-opened with the king, and in June 1648 the 11 conservative members whose impeachment the army had demanded in 1647 re-took their seats. In September, the House despatched commissioners to meet with the king on the Isle of Wight. When the army had done its work for parliament's safety, there was every prospect that its interests would be sacrificed in a new treaty between the parliamentary majority and the king.

However, the army had no intention of allowing this to happen, and it is at this point that the full significance of its politicisation in 1647 becomes apparent. In that year reservations regarding the king's reliability in any settlement had been made public, and the army had declared its right to a voice in any political settlement. Now it intended to exercise that right. The Second Civil War had greatly strengthened its position on both issues. Charles's negotiations with the Scots, his secret *Engagement*, his willingness to see a new war and a foreign invasion inflicted on his English subjects were, in the eyes of the army and a minority of MPs, final proof that he could not be trusted. Therefore they argued that it was pointless to negotiate any agreement with him, since he could not be relied upon to maintain it. More importantly, however, they claimed that he had not only forfeited the right to be trusted, he had also forfeited his right to be regarded as God's anointed – by rejecting God's verdict, revealed in his first defeat at parliament's hands, he had rejected God himself, destroyed his own divine status, and should be brought to account for his crimes like any ordinary man.

b) The Role of Religion: the Meaning of Providence

> **KEY ISSUES** What was Providence? How did belief in Providence influence events?

It is only if the impact of the Second Civil War is seen in relation to the widespread belief in God's Providence that its full significance can be understood. This belief that God directed human behaviour according to his Will and intention was by no means confined to religious radicals, although it was particularly intense among those with strong Puritan views. Men who wanted to dedicate their lives to God's service needed to know what God wanted them to do. Their method was to observe the pattern of events and try to work out how God was directing them, seeking in this an understanding of God's purpose and their own place in it. Once God's will was known, their duty was to pursue that purpose with all their strength. It was no coincidence that the army's declaration that Charles I had become a 'man of blood'; to be brought to account for his crimes, had come after a long prayer-meeting held at Windsor in April 1648. In this process they had sought to know the Will of God, and having apparently discovered it, to follow its direction.

This pattern of behaviour can be seen again and again in the life of Oliver Cromwell. Before any momentous decision, Cromwell was paralysed by inactivity, until a sign of some kind showed him which way God wished him to go. This was the case in June 1647, when his indecision over the army mutinies was brought to an end by the visit of Cornet Joyce, after which he pursued the army's cause with vigour and determination. At such times, considerations of legality, of conventional loyalties and duties, weighed little in the balance against what he saw as his duty to God. Thus he could justify resisting the legal authority of parliament and coercing the king. Therefore, the essential importance of the Second Civil War to men like Cromwell went beyond the issue of whether or not Charles could be trusted – by leading the king to renew the struggle and publicly fly in the face of God's verdict, God had placed Charles in conflict with his Will and made it the duty of his servants to bring the king to justice. By comparison, ordinary considerations of legality and respect for authority and kingship were of little importance.

This does not mean that the interpretation of God's will was easy. Cromwell himself agonised over the steps to be taken after the king's second defeat, as his letters of the autumn of 1648 reveal. It has been suggested that he lingered in Yorkshire on military business, while the campaign to bring Charles to justice was led by Ireton, precisely because of his uncertainty. In correspondence with his cousin, Robert Hammond, who was effectively the king's gaoler on the Isle of Wight, Cromwell debated the issue:

1 Dear Robin ... If thou wilt seek, seek to know the mind of God in all that chain of providence, whereby God brought thee thither, and that person [Charles I] to thee; how, before and since, God has ordered him, and affairs concerning him: and then tell me whether there be not
5 some glorious and high meaning in all this ...
    You say: God hath appointed authorities among the nations, to which active or passive obedience is to be yielded. This resides in

England in the parliament ... [In answer] to this, I...desire thee to see
what thou findest in thy own heart as to two or three plain consider-
10 ations. First, whether Salus Populi [the safety of the people] be a sound
position? Secondly, whether in the way in hand [parliament's new negotiations with the king] this be provided for, or is the whole fruit of the
war like to be frustrated, and all most like to turn to what it was or
worse? Thirdly, whether this army be not a lawful power, called by God
15 to oppose and fight against the king upon such stated grounds ...?
      But truly these kinds of reasonings may be but fleshly, either with or
against: only it is good to try what truth may be in them. And the Lord
teach us. My dear friend, let us look into providences; surely they mean
somewhat. They hang so together; have been so constant, so clear and
20 unclouded ...

What is clear from these letters is that Cromwell was not unaware of
the logical arguments for and against a settlement with the king, nor
of the dangers inherent in either path – but what is crucial is that, if
convinced that either policy was God's will, he would have little hesi-
tation in pursuing it. Hence the essential significance of the Second
Civil War was to convince some that Charles must be brought to justice because his crimes and his untrustworthiness merited it, and to
convince others that this must be done because it was the will of God
and their overriding duty. While both motives were important (and
not always distinguishable or separable) it was the latter that gave
social conservatives like Cromwell the stomach for revolution.

c) The Army's Case

> **KEY ISSUE** How did the army justify their call for the trial and
> punishment of the king?

While Cromwell debated in the North, the army's attack on the king
was orchestrated by Henry Ireton. His task was made easier by the
king, who dragged out negotiations with parliament's commissioners
and privately informed his friends that he would not regard himself
as bound by any 'mock-treaty'. In the meantime Ireton persuaded a
reluctant Fairfax that the army should have its say, and entered new
discussions with the Levellers – this time, however, the army was represented entirely by its officers. While these discussions continued, he
compiled a new Remonstrance which was presented to parliament as
the view of the army on 20 November.
      Its text is interesting, in that it combined both human and provi-
dential arguments against the king:

1 Where a person trusted with a limited power to rule according to laws
   and ... with express covenant and oath also [the king's coronation oath]
   obliged to preserve and protect the rights and liberties of the people,

for, and by whom he is entrusted shall not only pervert that trust and
5 abuse that power ... but also ... rise to the assuming of hurtful powers
which he never had committed to him, and indeed take away all those
foundations of right and liberty, and of redress or remedy too ... and
shall fly to the way of force upon his trusting people and attempt by it
to uphold and establish himself in that absolute tyrannical power ...
10 such a person, in so doing, does forfeit all that trust and power he had;
and absolving the people from the bonds of covenant and peace betwixt
him and them, does set them free to take their best advantage, and, if
he fall within their power, to proceed in judgement against him, even
for that alone, if there were no more.

However, the Remonstrance continued, there was much more to be
brought against Charles. As Derek Hirst summarised, 'the king had
repeatedly broken his contract with [the people], and God had
repeatedly witnessed against him' [*Authority and Conflict*, p. 285].
While the document called for him to be brought to justice, it did not,
however, argue for the complete abolition of monarchy. That act
would be justified later in works such as John Milton's *Tenure of Kings
and Magistrates* (1649) after the step had already been taken. Hirst has
suggested that this caution was dictated by Cromwell's reluctance to
consider such a step, but it may have been Ireton's own preference
for keeping possible options open. The need to remove Charles was
clear; how to replace him was another matter.

The army was given little opportunity to debate this matter. While
its remonstrances were ignored, the parliamentary majority pushed
ahead with the proposed treaty with the king. In early December the
commissioners returned from the Isle of Wight with the king's answer
to four bills, and although he had rejected parliament's proposals
regarding the Church, the conservatives were heartened by his concessions over the militia. On 5 December the House of Commons
voted that his answers were sufficient basis for further negotiations.
This was undoubtedly a prelude to his return to London and a rapid
settlement. Seeing their concerns and interests ignored and about to
be sacrificed, the army acted. Ireton wished to dissolve the House of
Commons and hold new elections on a reformed franchise. He was
dissuaded from this by the radical MPs, such as the republicans
Thomas Scot and Edmund Ludlow, who had now aligned themselves
with the army. They argued that a military intervention would be
unpopular and that elections would probably go against them. It was
decided, therefore, to purge the present parliament, and leave the
settlement in the hands of the minority who would be left.

d) The Attitudes of MPs

> **KEY ISSUE** What factors influenced MPs into supporting or opposing the execution of the king?

The participation of a minority of MPs in this process, and the determination of others to settle with the king despite his untrustworthiness and minimal concessions, raises some interesting questions about the different parliamentary factions and their motivations. Attempts to label groups of MPs as Presbyterians and Independents, or radicals and republicans, tend to disguise as much as they reveal, and we cannot simply assume that all MPs who acted in a particular way did so for the same reasons. Nevertheless, there were deep and serious divisions among MPs about how to proceed, and the army certainly thought they could tell their friends from their enemies when they forcibly excluded the latter from parliament. An interesting and impressive attempt to study the views and motivations of different MPs was carried out by David Underdown in his study of Pride's Purge, published in 1971. Using the votes registered by MPs themselves and the lists of members excluded by the army, Underdown divided the Commons into five groups on the basis of how they acted and reacted to the trial and execution of the king. These were:

- 71 Revolutionaries, who actively supported the trial and execution;
- 83 Conformists, who accepted the event and participated in parliament thereafter;
- 86 Abstainers, who were not excluded by the army, but who chose to stay away from parliament in order to dissociate themselves from the action against the king;
- 186 Secluded MPs who were excluded from parliament by the army because they had supported the treaty with the king; and
- 45 imprisoned MPs, who were imprisoned by the army because they were seen as the strongest supporters of the agreement with the king.

Underdown then investigated the lives, circumstances and attitudes of these MPs, in order to evaluate the characteristics and motives that led them to act as they did. His conclusions reinforce Derek Hirst's arguments regarding the fluidity of parliamentary factions and the complex considerations that led MPs to act in a particular way. Party labels are rarely relevant, and are often confusing. More recently, however, Underdown's figures have been used as the basis of statistical analysis on computer, and while this also supports the argument that MPs could not be divided into clear-cut parties, it has produced some broad conclusions that may indicate something of MPs' motives and considerations. In many cases the evidence is limited and fragmented, and there are many MPs whose attitudes simply remain unknown.

However, in comparing particular characteristics across the five groups of MPs, two interesting points stand out. In general terms, the Secluded and Imprisoned MPs who supported the treaty with the king were of higher social status and income than those who supported the king's execution. This might help to explain their determination to defend both the existing political system and the structure of society by retaining a powerful monarchy and a state church. But it would be dangerous to pursue this line too far for the difference is not great – all MPs were members of the governing classes, and there was a significant number of the most wealthy and important members who associated themselves with the 'revolution' in some way. The second point is more clear-cut. Among the Revolutionaries and Conformists who supported or acquiesced in the trial and execution, a large number are known to have held strong, and often radical religious views.

Again, the generalisation should not be taken too far. The religious views of many MPs are unrecorded, and not all revolutionaries can be shown to have been influenced by religion. Nevertheless, individual case studies have shown that many of the wealthiest and most important supporters of the revolution had strong religious views which perhaps outweighed their social and political reservations. Therefore, it seems that it can be said with confidence that this evidence enhances the importance of the religious issues and attitudes that have been put forward above as significant factors in bringing about the execution of the king. It could further be suggested that wealth and social status had a negative importance, tending to incline MPs against radical solutions and in favour of defending the existing system, while religious commitment exercised a positive effect, causing some MPs to act in a revolutionary, or radical way even against their own material interests. What is clearest of all is that, in describing how MPs divided over the issue of settlement, we are not looking at coherent parties or even factions, but at men who shared many of the same beliefs and concerns and who made individual decisions in the light of a number of, often conflicting, influences and considerations.

Few men demonstrate these complex and conflicting motivations more clearly than the supposed 'arch-revolutionary', Oliver Cromwell. The tone of his letter to Robert Hammond (quoted on pp. 131–2) and his delay in returning to London are indications of his uncertainty and the conflicting considerations that influenced his decisions. On 6 December the parliament buildings were surrounded by troops from the regiment of Colonel Pride. MPs who were classified as being conservative were excluded, and others, hearing of what was happening, chose to stay away. The most prominent supporters of the proposed treaty were imprisoned, although Denzil Holles had been warned and had already left the country. Initially, those who chose to enter the Commons had difficulty in establishing a quorum of forty, but in the following weeks more MPs returned, partly as a result of persuasion by Cromwell. He had reached London on 7 December and declared his support for the purge. However, it was by no means certain that he had yet decided in favour of bringing the king to trial, and he continued to counsel caution until the end of the month. Nor was he alone in this. It is often assumed that Pride's Purge was a deliberate step towards the king's trial and execution, but it is worth remembering that the timing had been dictated by parliament rather than the army, and that the purge was in some ways a defensive step, intended to prevent the majority in parliament from, as the army saw it, betraying themselves and their cause.

e) The Execution of the King

> **KEY ISSUE** Why was Charles executed in January 1649?

However, if the die was not cast at the time of the purge, the remaining days of December completed the process. Cromwell still hesitated, and seems to have attempted to persuade Charles to make some meaningful concessions, but the king refused. This may well have been interpreted by Cromwell as the sign from God that he had been waiting for; thereafter he seems to have pushed forward the trial and its inevitable conclusion with all speed. He was determined that, if Charles was to be removed, it would be by public trial, with charges openly brought and justified. If such a trial were to take place, however, there could be no doubt of its outcome. Acquittal would leave the problems of settlement even less capable of solution. Once found guilty, Charles would have to be executed. It was clear that he would never agree to abdicate, imprisonment would leave him free to plot and foment further rebellions, and overseas exile would simply invite him to raise a new army and return.

That still did not mean that the abolition of the monarchy had to follow. A minority of MPs had now committed themselves to republicanism, but many of those who were not prepared to see the return of Charles Stuart had no such commitment, and the views of the army officers seemed mixed. On 23 December a meeting of MPs discussed various means of replacing Charles. It was recorded by Bulstrode Whitelocke, one of the 'Rump' of MPs who remained in the House of Commons after Pride's Purge.

1   Sir Thomas Widdrington and I went together, according to appointment to the Speaker's house. There we met various gentlemen of the House, and we consulted about settling the kingdom by the parliament, and not to leave all to the sword ... Some of them were wholly against
5   any king at all; others were against having the present king, or his eldest son or his second son to be king; others were for the third son, the Duke of Gloucester (who was among them and might be educated as

they should appoint) to be made king. They came, after a long debate, to no resolution at all.

Cromwell and some officers had similar views to these MPs, but many of the officers favoured a republican solution. Nevertheless, it was two months after the king's execution that the step was finally taken to end the monarchy and establish the republican Commonwealth. It is difficult to escape the conclusion that the overriding reason for the abolition of the monarchy was the lack of a viable replacement for Charles. There was simply no acceptable or safe candidate for the throne.

On 1 January 1649 the Rump agreed to establish a High Court to try the king; the remaining Lords objected, but the Rump simply declared the Commons able to make law without them. The king's trial opened on 20 January, with John Bradshaw as Lord President of the Court. Charles was brought in, and the charge read; he had tried, it was claimed 'to erect and uphold in himself an unlimited and tyrannical power to rule according to his will and to overthrow the rights and liberties of the people'. He had waged war on the parliament, granted commissions to Irish rebels, and was thus responsible for all the death, damage and destruction thereby created. Charles responded with dignity. Claiming to have received his trust from God, he denied that the court had any right to try him, and refused to plead. With strength and courage he declared that 'I do stand more for the liberty of my people than any here that come to be my pretended judges. And therefore let me know by what lawful authority I am seated here, and I will answer it. Otherwise I will not answer it.' When the verdict was returned and sentenced pronounced, he tried to speak, but was denied the right. 'I am not suffered to speak', he declared 'expect what justice other people will have'. When the sentence was carried out on 30 January, eyewitnesses described the 'mighty groan' that came from the people present.

There is little doubt that Charles served the cause of monarchy better by his death than he ever had in his life. The publication and massive sales of Eikon Basilike, supposedly the dead king's memoirs written during his last days, fed the myth of martyrdom, but Charles himself had laid the groundwork by his courage and dignity in death, and by the force of his argument. However justified Cromwell and his allies might feel in the eyes of God, they had behaved illegally in the eyes of the law, and continued to do so. This was to be the fatal flaw and weakness that undermined all their efforts to achieve a stable regime thereafter, and led ultimately to the restoration of the monarchy in 1660. Yet for all his admirable qualities in these last days, a dispassionate examination of what brought Charles to that position must surely find that, for whatever reason or principle, he himself had been the greatest single cause of his own trial and execution.

Working on Chapter 6

Making Notes on Chapter 6

Before investigating the causes of the king's execution in 1649, you will find it useful to consolidate your understanding of the material contained in this chapter by making notes on the events of 1648–9 and analysing the attitudes and ideas that influenced their outcome. Use the following headings to organise your notes:

The Execution of the King.

1. The Second Civil War
   a) military significance
   b) political effects – distrust of the king – ideas/attitudes, belief in Providence
2. Trial and Execution
   a) attempts at settlement
   b) Pride's Purge
   c) attitudes and motives
   d) the king's death

Given their importance in the final outcome, it would be useful to explore more fully the beliefs and attitudes of those who supported the king's execution. You would therefore find it helpful to answer the following source-based questions before proceeding further.

Source-based questions on Chapter 6

1 The Role of Providence.

Re-read Cromwell's letter to Robert Hammond, printed on pp. 131–2 and answer the following questions.

a) What events might Cromwell consider to be the "chain of providence" that had brought Charles into Hammond's care? [Interpretation in context] 4 marks
b) Who does he believe to be in control of those events? [inference] 1 mark
c) What "glorious and high meaning" could these events imply? [interpretation in context] 3 marks
d) What does Cromwell mean by the term "Salus Populi" and whether it "be provided for" in parliament's negotiations? [comprehension] 3 marks
e) On what basis could the army be considered "a lawful power"? [interpretation in context] 3 marks
f) Cromwell later dismisses these considerations as "fleshly reasonings" What does he mean by this? [interpretation in context] 3 marks

g) What does Cromwell expect Hammond to do when he advises him to "look into providences? [interpretation in context] *3 marks*

h) In the light of these statements, explain Cromwell's belief in Providence and how it might influence his actions. [synthesis] *5 marks*

Now re-read the Army's Remonstrance, written by Ireton. (pp. 132–3)

i) What arguments does Ireton use to justify the king's trial? [comprehension/inference] *3 marks*

j) In what ways do these arguments differ from those put forward by Cromwell? Do they conflict? [comparison and cross-reference] *4 marks*

k) In what ways do the nature of these two documents help to explain their different emphasis? [Cross-reference, evaluation] *4 marks*

l) Using the evidence of these sources and all the information that you have gathered, explain why some officers and MPs believed that the king should be brought to trial in 1648–9. [synthesis] *14 marks*

The final section of this chapter is intended to address a major issue of the period, and to offer an example of essay writing based on the interaction of causal factors. The approach is indicated by brief section headings, and it is intended that, as you read the essay, you should be able to compile a list of causal factors to provide you with a basis for approaching a range of different essay questions on this topic.

Answering essay questions on 'The Execution of Charles I'

You can use either a causal structure similar to the section above, or the 'hypothesis-testing' approach, whichever seems more appropriate for a particular question. You should then choose one essay to write.

1. 'The most important cause of the execution of Charles I was Charles himself.' How far do you agree?

2. How far can the execution of Charles I be explained by reference to the actions of the army and its supporters?

3. 'Although it could not be foreseen at the time, the execution of Charles I was inevitable from the time of his defeat in 1646.' Do you agree?

4. How far can the execution of Charles I be described as a revolutionary act?

5. 'The execution of Charles I cannot be understood without studying the religious outlook of his contemporaries.' How far would you agree?

Conclusion: 'Why was Charles I executed in 1649?'

1 Introduction

(Use to analyse the question and establish issues to be addressed.) The execution of Charles I was an event without parallel in Europe before the French Revolution of 1789. It was not unknown for inadequate monarchs to be deposed, and even murdered, but to bring an anointed monarch to public trial, to condemn him to death and to justify this in the name of the people was unprecedented. The event requires explanation because it was revolutionary, and it can be argued that an event of such significance can only be explained by long-term changes in the nature of society, its beliefs and attitudes. However, the continuing search for a settlement after 1646 could offer the alternative view that the trial and execution of the king was the unexpected and unintended result of errors and misjudgements in the crucial years of 1646–9.

2 The Conditional Factors

An examination of English society in the century before the Civil War does reveal a number of significant changes and developments. The Reformation had established religious doctrines which emphasised the importance of individual faith and interpretation. The immediate effect was to create conflict within the Church and to make the monarch directly responsible for these divisive issues. The long-term result was to undermine authority in religion and encourage separatism. In addition, the development of the concept of King-in-parliament as the supreme power in the state increased the status and significance of parliament at a time when social and economic changes (to which the Reformation also contributed) were increasing the numbers and wealth of the gentry who dominated the House of Commons. Protestant reforms ended the clerical monopoly of education and produced a more educated and articulate laity; and at the higher social levels these qualities were encouraged by the growing reliance upon the gentry in government and administration. Combined with the financial problems of the monarchy, these conditions created tensions and stresses within the structure of government, which, if badly handled, could develop into open conflict.

Yet there is little evidence in the events leading up to war in 1642 of any desire to make radical changes in the system of government, let alone to remove the monarch as the centre of power. Those who led the struggle against Charles I were seeking to resist infringements of their rights and privileges, and to secure a reformed Protestant Church. What was radical in their behaviour was their willingness to change the balance of the constitution in order to achieve these objectives. It is therefore difficult to argue that long-term changes in social structure, political practice or even political thinking played any significant part in bringing about the revolutionary act of executing Charles I, except in so far as they helped to bring about the Civil War that was its essential pre-condition.

It was, in fact, the war itself that did most to create the potential for revolution. Faced with the need to justify military action, parliament's apologists evolved more radical political theories in claiming the right to rebel against a monarch who abused his powers. To justify their role, they claimed that parliament represented the people, for whose safety and well-being government was created. In 1646 these arguments were extended by the Levellers into a doctrine of the sovereignty of the people, and in 1649 they formed the basis of the charge of treason upon which the king was tried and condemned. In the conditions of war, theory tended to follow practice, and each step moved in a more radical direction.

This was partly the result of the war's impact in other areas, especially its effect on religious ideas and practice. The crisis between king and parliament that developed in 1641 revealed the existence of religious radicals whose separatist organisation, lay preaching and demands for some form of religious toleration undermined authority in church and state. It is clear from their rapid emergence in 1641–2 that these groups were in existence before 1640. They originated in the Protestant insistence on an individual, Bible-based faith, but they had remained few and scattered. With the collapse of censorship in 1641 they were able to declare their existence and publish their ideas. Open debate allowed their ideas to develop, and wartime conditions gave them credibility. The conflict between king and parliament reinforced millenarian ideas of a struggle between good and evil which was reaching its climax in England. In these circumstances, separatist congregations increased and a demand for some measure of religious toleration was formulated. The need to campaign for such rights led to demands for freedom of speech and of the press. Political conflict, economic dislocation, religious enthusiasm and militant individualism gave rise to a range of radical ideas, culminating in the democratic republicanism of the Levellers. Perhaps most significant of all, in the New Model Army and its leaders radicals found sympathy and protection. By 1646 the needs and conditions of war had released, if not created, genuinely revolutionary forces within English society.

These developments did not, however, make the king's execution inevitable, or even likely at this stage. Radical ideas were held only by a tiny minority, and the separatists included many members like Cromwell and Ireton, whose political and social attitudes were otherwise conventional. When Charles surrendered in 1646, it was assumed that he would bow to the logic of defeat, and accept a negotiated settlement. This was certainly the aim of both parliament and the army leaders in 1646 and throughout 1647. It was the failure to find this settlement that opened the way to a more radical solution.

The most obvious reason for this failure is the king's refusal to accept any of the propositions put to him. In 1646–7 he rejected the *Newcastle Propositions* offered by parliament and later the *Heads of the Proposals* offered by the army. His reluctance to come to terms arose partly from his convictions regarding kingship and his role and power in Church and State. For Charles, kingship was a divinely appointed trust, and to accept any significant reduction of his role would be a failure to do his duty. Similarly, he regarded his right to govern the

Church through the ancient institution of bishops as both a social and religious obligation. These matters were not, in fact, negotiable.

In this context, Charles was prepared to delay, to prevaricate, or to make short-term concessions, but genuine agreement was not his intention. What encouraged his strategy was the obvious fragmentation of his enemies. In 1646 there were fears among the English parliamentary leaders that Charles would come to an agreement with their Scottish allies, based upon the imposition of a Presbyterian church system in England in return for the re-establishment of his legal and constitutional powers. By the end of the year this danger had faded, but had been replaced by growing concern at the activities of the radical minority and, in particular, their influence within the parliamentary army. The determination of Holles and the Derby House Committee to remove the radical threat, by disbanding the army, backfired and by May/June 1647 the army was in open revolt. Most crucially of all, the leading officers like Cromwell (and to a lesser extent, Fairfax) had placed army unity above their loyalty to parliament, effectively creating a third political force to complicate the process of settlement.

The politicisation of the army was thus brought about by conservative errors, but its effect was to give a new influence to the radical forces released by the war. In many ways, events had conspired to gather these forces around the army. Its rapid success against the royalist forces had encouraged the belief that such victories were the work of Providence, and that the army was the instrument of God's will. The conservative attack on the army in 1647 had forged a new religious and political unity within its ranks. While the army was not politically representative in any legal or constitutional sense, it did speak on behalf of a section of the population and, in its own eyes, represented God's people and His cause. Hence it was justified in intervening in the process of settlement to protect interests which would otherwise be overlooked and ignored. Its purpose at this stage was to influence the nature of an agreement with the king, not to depose him. In different circumstances, however, it might be capable of contemplating radical solutions if those interests were at risk.

In the short term, these events seemed to work to the advantage of the king. Throughout 1647 he played off the army and parliament against each other, and when this failed to produce satisfactory terms, he was able to exploit Scottish fears to renew the war. In December 1647 the Scots signed an Engagement by which they would invade England to restore the king in return for a (temporary) Presbyterian settlement of the Church. Motivated by religious zeal and dislike of radicalism, they were no longer content to leave the matter of settlement to the English. Although this Second Civil War had little military importance, its political significance was immense. Royalist risings in England revealed the extent of popular support for a settlement with the king, strengthening conservative desires for a rapid return to traditional government. At the

same time, the war convinced the army and its supporters that a settlement with the king was impossible and created, for the first time, a real
possibility that they would seek a settlement without him.

By the autumn of 1648, therefore, parliament's supporters were
more deeply divided than ever. Fear of radicalism and the threat
represented by radical groups, as well as resentment of the army's
interference in political matters, was deep-rooted among the
majority of MPs and the governing class that they represented.
Although the parliamentary majority voted in January 1648 against
further negotiations with the king who had so clearly betrayed their
trust, they were in fact incapable of visualising any other solution.
Belief in a social hierarchy which was defended and maintained by
monarchy, and fears of social disintegration if the controlling influence of Church and King was weakened meant that, ultimately, they
depended on the king's co-operation in any settlement. When
Charles told the parliamentary commissioners in 1647 that 'without
me you will fall', he was stating what they believed, as well as his own
convictions. When the Second Civil War ended in the early autumn
of 1648, the parliamentary majority saw no option other than the
renewal of negotiations, even at the cost of significant concessions to
the king.

The army and its supporters disagreed. Charles's cynical betrayal of
those who sought to negotiate with him had finally convinced many
of them that no settlement could be secure because Charles could not
be trusted to maintain it. His willingness to break promises which he
regarded as extorted from him could be traced back to the *Petition of
Right* in 1628, and these betrayals contributed to the distrust that had
now reached new heights. In this context, the Second Civil War provided final and undeniable proof that Charles was unfit to govern. An
army *Remonstrance*, written by Henry Ireton and presented to parliament on 20 November declared that he had betrayed his trust and
that the nation's representatives had a duty to depose him for the
nation's safety. These views were supported by a minority of republican MPs, such as Sir Arthur Haselrig and Henry Marten. Drawing on
classical examples and parliament's own justification for taking up
arms, they justified the king's trial in political terms, and saw the
Second Civil War as proof of his betrayal.

For others, particularly the army leaders, the influence of religion
was more important. Desire for a measure of toleration 'for tender
consciences' to meet outside the confines of the national Church was
a consideration, as was the desire for a 'godly reformation' that
depended on reform of the Church. More influential in this context
was the widespread and intense belief in the role of God's providence
in human affairs, which interpreted the victory of parliament in 1646
as God's verdict on the struggle, and the instrument of victory, the
New Model Army as having been called by God to defend his cause.
When Charles renewed the war in 1648, he was not merely betraying

his trust, he was rejecting the will of God and thereby forfeiting the divine status accorded to a Christian monarch. When God made him behave in this way it could only signify that God had abandoned him – it was therefore the duty of those who wished to serve God to bring the man, Charles Stuart, to justice.

By December 1648, therefore, a combination of conditional factors had made the trial and execution of Charles I likely, but not yet certain. The impact of the war on extreme Protestant beliefs had created radical forces, capable of radical solutions. These could have been contained if king and parliament had been able to conclude an agreement in 1646–7, but Charles's character and beliefs made this impossible. The Second Civil War, initiated by the king, had convinced these radical forces that he ought to be brought to justice, because there was no alternative and because it was the will of God. At this point, however, the outcome was still uncertain. In the first place, the radicals did not, apparently, have the full support of Cromwell, who seems to have deliberately remained in Yorkshire on military duties. Secondly, the army petitions seem to have been intended to persuade rather than coerce the parliamentary majority, and it is unlikely that they would ever have succeeded. It was clearly within the power of the army leaders to impose a settlement of their choice, but the ability to impose a settlement did not necessarily provide the will to do so. The army leaders hesitated to take such a revolutionary step, and it was the actions of the conservatives in parliament, and of the king himself, that finally brought it about.

3 The Contingent Factors

What sparked off the final crisis was the determination of parliamentary conservatives to conclude an agreement with the king that would enable them to destroy the radical threat. On 5 December they voted the king's replies to their latest offers to be a suitable basis for negotiation. The threat of a conservative settlement, betraying all that they had fought for, forced the army to act on 6 December and to purge parliament. Pride's Purge, retrospectively approved by Cromwell, was the beginning of the process by which Charles was brought to trial, but its timing was dictated by conservative initiatives rather than the army. Even then, Cromwell seems to have tried to find a compromise solution, to persuade Charles to make some concession. The king's refusal seems to have finally convinced Cromwell that trial and execution were the will of God, after which he supported the process with energy and determination. Once the trial began, there could be no doubt about the verdict and sentence. To acquit Charles was unthinkable, and to leave him alive, in prison or in exile, would simply enable him to initiate new wars and invasions. If Charles could not return to his throne on terms which ensured the security of the opposition and their cause, his trial and execution were the only other viable option.

4 Conclusion – the Relative Importance of Different Factors

It is clear that many different factors played a part in bringing about the execution of Charles I in 1649, with varying degrees of significance. One way of evaluating the significance of these factors is to consider how the necessary combination built up, to the point where the execution of the king became the most likely outcome of the situation. Religious and political conflicts, including radical religious ideas and heightened by the personality of the king, existed in 1646, but there was no suggestion that he should be removed, let alone tried and executed. Hence, although these factors created the preconditions that allowed the king's execution, they cannot be sufficient in themselves to explain it. The death of Charles was not the inevitable result of underlying social, religious or political changes. By the autumn of 1648, however, a large section of the army and some MPs had become convinced that the king could, and should, be brought to account. Moreover, when the parliamentary majority ignored their views, they felt justified in overriding the law, the rights of parliament and popular opinion in order to impose them. It required provocation by parliamentary conservatives to finally force them into action, but given the attitudes of conservative MPs and the king's aims, this was almost bound to happen. Hence the key factors lie in three developments which occurred between the end of 1646 and the autumn of 1648. The first was the politicisation of the army, creating a political force which was capable of revolutionary action. The second was the king's continuing refusal to come to a workable settlement, removing all viable alternatives. The third was the Second Civil War and Charles's responsibility for it, which both demonstrated the need for a radical solution and provided its justification. It can thus be said that it was the interaction of these factors, in the context of changing attitudes produced by war and upheaval, which brought about the king's execution.

Ultimately two factors were crucial. Long term political, social and religious developments were not necessarily revolutionary but they created the conditions of war and upheaval in which revolutionary forces could take shape, and the existence of these radical forces was essential for the final outcome. Yet it was the errors and miscalculations of Charles and his parliamentary opponents that enabled, or drove, this revolutionary minority to take action. Their refusal to accommodate the interests of the radical minority, particularly in religion, created a new political force around the army. The king's continued and stubborn rejection of God's will and cause left no room for compromise. In 1642 his intransigence led to war, in 1646 to stalemate; in the changed conditions of 1649, it led to his own downfall, and that of the monarchy itself.

7 Conclusion; War, Rebellion and Revolution

> **KEY ISSUE** Were the Civil Wars a Great Rebellion, or a Revolution?

The nature of the upheavals known collectively as the Civil Wars has been the subject of considerable debate among historians, as it was among contemporaries. This is, in part, because of the complexity of the subject matter. There is, for example disagreement as to the number and dates of the wars. If we consider the English Civil Wars, there are two – dating from 1642–6, and in 1648. However, if we accept the arguments of Conrad Russell that events in England cannot be explained in isolation and that we should be considering the Civil Wars in a British context, then they begin in 1637 with the so-called Scottish Rebellion, and end in 1651 when Cromwell defeated Charles II at the head of a Scottish army at Worcester.

Similarly, our judgements may be influenced by the focus that we give to political events. Historians concerned with explaining the outbreak of war in 1642 are far less likely to view it as a 'revolution' than those who focus primarily on its outcome – the undeniably revolutionary act of executing a crowned monarch in the name of his people. If the focus is extended to 1660, and the return of the monarchy, then judgements may well require further revision. What this means is that all such judgements made by historians are essentially interpretations of the available evidence, defined by the nature of the questions asked and the perspective applied. As such, they were also affected by the attitudes and interests of the historians themselves.

From the outset, explanations of the Civil War and its causes have been influenced by the political views of their authors. For Lord Clarendon, who as Edward Hyde was the leader of a moderate royalist group in the Long Parliament and who later became chief adviser to Charles II, the war was a Great Rebellion, borne out of a crisis created by a Puritan faction who wanted to force Charles to adopt their policies in Church and state. On the other hand, Thomas May (1595–1650) who was one of the Long Parliament's secretaries, wrote two accounts – *The History of the Parliament of England* (1647) and *A Breviary of the History of the Parliament of England* (1650) in which the blame for the crisis, the outbreak of war and the abolition of the monarchy was laid firmly at the door of Charles I. These accounts set the tone for those that followed.

With the development of a parliamentary monarchy after the removal of the Catholic king: James II in the Glorious Revolution of 1688–9; the parliamentarian viewpoint began to take precedence, and a Whig interpretation of history began to take shape. In this view the Civil War was part of a struggle for political liberty and the Protestant religion against the attempt by Charles I and his sons to establish absolute monarchy and a Catholic tyranny – a Puritan Revolution. Although this interpretation did not go completely unchallenged, by the nineteenth century it had become an established view that could be applied by contemporaries in different ways. For most, like the historian and nineteenth-century politician, Macaulay, it formed the basis on which to demonstrate the virtues of parliamentary government as developed in Britain and America.

All these interpretations unashamedly drew on history to influence contemporary political struggles. Macaulay, for example, made no attempt at a balanced interpretation of characters or events, and was content to portray James II as nothing less than a Catholic tyrant. However, the nineteenth-century development of scientific study, with its rules of evidence and experimental proof, and the spread of education and new educational institutions created a generation of historians, who took pride in 'scientific' methods and professional objectivity. Claiming to avoid political standpoints and to base their conclusions on the objective study of documentary evidence, historians such as S.R. Gardiner in his *History of England, 1603–56* (1883–4) provided the first modern historical accounts of the Civil War as well as the model and methodology upon which modern historical study is based. What they did not provide, however, was a radically new interpretation of the Civil War. In the words of R.C. Richardson in his *The Debate on the English Revolution Revisited* (1991), 'Scientific history did not destroy the Whig interpretation of history; it merely diluted it'. Gardiner and his colleagues might attempt to establish a balanced view, but they could not escape from their own perceptions of good and evil and their Victorian liberal upbringing. This had given them a liberal view of 'progress' in which they perceived history as the story of the development of political liberty from primitive society to the pinnacle of late nineteenth-century Britain.

In the twentieth century, however, their focus on political and religious issues was challenged as being too narrow, particularly by socialist or 'Marxist' historians who saw history as a class struggle. Influenced by R.H. Tawney's *Religion and the Rise of Capitalism*, published in 1926, they interpreted the Civil Wars as a struggle between a rising capitalist gentry and merchant class, and an older feudal nobility led by the king, who tried to hold back change and maintain their power and privileges. Hence the Puritan Revolution became the English Revolution. In turn, this interpretation was challenged as being too simplistic, by historians who investigated individuals and localities in greater depth and detail, or who extended the perspective spatially across Britain. In recent years the range of research has widened, extended, and revisited older views, so that whatever explanation of the seventeenth-century crisis is advanced, there will be arguments to challenge it. What has become clear from this welter of debate, is that no simple, single-issue explanation of such complex events can be sufficient.

The results of these enquiries can be summarised in three main categories. The 'Whig' view argues that the crisis of 1640 was caused by long-term political and religious problems, which made some kind of political conflict, if not a war, almost inevitable. The Civil Wars were part of a struggle for political and religious freedom. The Marxist view is similar, but places emphasis on social and economic causes rather than religion and politics. In both cases the wars are seen to arise from fundamental problems in government and society and to involve serious ideological differences, so that conflict of some kind and major changes as a result, were probably unavoidable. Hence the Civil Wars are portrayed as a revolution. Those who challenge these theories have been labelled 'revisionist' historians, acknowledging the existence of problems that Charles inherited, but arguing that these were manageable, and that crisis, war and revolution were by no means likely, let alone inevitable outcomes. The Civil Wars were therefore the result of errors and misunderstandings, the work of individuals rather than of great underlying causes. They may be characterised as a conspiracy, a rebellion or an accident, but not as a revolution.

Inevitably such simplistic categories fail to reflect the range and variation of views within them, but serve as a broad indication of approach. More importantly, they reflect the fact that the debate is ongoing – each view has its defenders, and the response to new argument is not to abandon older interpretations but to refine and develop them to accommodate new evidence. The central process of historical enquiry involves acquiring an understanding of existing scholarship, and evaluating it against the available evidence. When judgements stand up to such testing they are strengthened, where they do not they are adjusted. Where views conflict, the differences need to be explained, and sometimes reconciled. By these means, historical understanding develops, and a balanced synthesis will often emerge. The most effective conclusion to this volume, therefore, will be the one that you form for yourself by using the final 'working on' section below to analyse and evaluate a range of historians' views in the light of your own knowledge and the evidence that you have acquired from it.

Working on Chapter 7

Evaluating different historians' interpretations is an essential part of AS and A2 study, which brings together the techniques required for handling sources and demonstrating an understanding of historical content and concepts. At the best levels, it requires an understanding that all historical judgements are provisional and partial, and an ability to construct, maintain and defend a balanced judgement on this basis. To draw your own conclusions on the nature of the Civil Wars, you should:

- Read and analyse the sources below, and list their main claims and arguments as a brief statement;
- Use the sources and your own knowledge to test [i.e. support and challenge] these statements.
- Where testing reveals a weakness in the statement, or suggests that it should be extended, offer an adjusted version.
- Where statements appear to be in conflict, consider whether the conflict can be reconciled.
- Finally, use the evidence from the sources, your own knowledge, and the ideas developed from your testing to explain how far you would accept the claim that the Civil Wars and execution of Charles I constituted a revolution.

From G. Huehns [ed.], *Clarendon: Selections from the History of the Rebellion and Civil Wars in England*, pp. 133, 215–16.

1 Mr Pym was looked upon as the man of greatest experience in parliament. . . . [He was]known to be inclined to the puritan party, though not of those furious resolutions against the Church as [some] others. [He was] wholly devoted to the Earl of Bedford, who had nothing of that
5 spirit . . . [and] was of too great and plentiful a fortune to wish subversion of the government; and it quickly appeared that he only intended to make himself and his friends great at Court, not at all to lessen the Court itself. . . .
    The lord Viscount Saye . . . had the deepest hand in the original con-
10 trivance of all the calamities which befell this unhappy kingdom, though he had not the least thought of dissolving the monarchy, and less of levelling the ranks and distinctions of men. For no man valued himself more upon his title, or had more ambition to make it greater, and to raise his fortune, which was but moderate for his title . . . He had always
15 great credit and authority in parliament . . . and was in truth the pilot that steered all those vessels which were freighted with sedition to destroy the government.

From C.H. Firth [ed.], *Memoirs of Edmund Ludlow*, Vol.1 pp. 37–8. Ludlow's father was an MP in 1640, and Edmund succeeded him as MP for Wiltshire in 1646. He became a staunch republican, signed the king's death warrant, and was a member of the Rump Parliament in 1649–53. He survived the Restoration but was forced into exile in 1662, where he wrote his memoirs. They were published in 1698–9 as part of a campaign to limit the king's military powers.

1 The nation was driven to a necessity of arming in defence of the laws, openly and frequently violated by the King; who had made it the chief business of his reign to invade the rights and privileges of the people, raising taxes by various arts without their consent in parliament;

5 encouraging and promoting a formal and superstitious clergy, discouraging the sober and virtuous amonst them … And knowing that parliaments were the most likely means of rectifying what was amiss … had endeavoured either to prevent their meeting, or to render them fruitless to the people, and only serviceable to his corrupt ends in granting
10 him money to carry on his harmful designs: a parliament now being called, it was clear that the king would do nothing effectual to redress the present, or secure the people from future mischiefs, choosing rather to contend with them by arms … I thought it my duty … to enter into the service of my country in the army commanded by the
15 earl of Essex under the authority of parliament.

From C. Hill, 'A Bourgeois Revolution?' in J.G.A. Pocock [ed.], *Three British Revolutions: 1641,1688, 1776,* p. 112.

1 By 1640 the social forces let loose by, or accompanying, the rise of capitalism, especially in agriculture, could no longer be contained within the old political framework except by means of a violent repression of which Charles I's government proved incapable. Among the 'social
5 forces accompanying the rise of capitalism' we must include not only the individualism of those who wished to make money by doing what they would with their own, but also the individualism of those who wished to follow their own consciences in worshipping God, and whose consciences led them to challenge the institutions of a stratified, hier-
10 archical society …

From A. Fletcher, *The Outbreak of the English Civil War,* pp. 407–9, 413, 415.

1 Great events do not necessarily have great causes, though it is natural for historians to seek them. Most of those who rode up to Westminster in November 1640 had no concept of a parliamentary cause in their minds. Reconciliation and settlement were seen as the purposes of par-
5 liaments and the reforms that most MPs envisaged seemed perfectly compatible with such an end. Only Pym and a few close friends saw the matter in totally different terms: for them the parliamentary cause was the rooting out of a conspiracy that struck at the core of the nation's life. Parliament's propaganda related every royal action between January
10 and November 1642 to this papist conspiracy … Their fundamental misconception of the political situation must surely be the starting point for an explanation of how war came about.…

    … This, though is only one side of the picture. Charles I [held] … a jaundiced view of parliaments and a strong sense of distrust of certain
15 individuals who he believed were ready to challenge his monarchy for private and selfish ends.… The king's misunderstanding of his opponents' aims would have been less serious if his character had been different. He was a man who magnified distrust even in the most loyal hearts …

    What happened in 1641 and 1642 was that two groups of men became
20 the prisoners of competing myths that fed on one another, so that

events seemed to confirm two opposing interpretations of the political crisis that were both originally misconceived and erroneous.

From C. Russell, *The Causes of the English Civil War,* pp. 212–13, and *The Crisis of Parliaments,* pp. 376–7.

1 The Civil War should be ascribed to a conjunction of seven events and non-events: why there were Bishops' Wars, why England lost them, why there was no political settlement in England, why the Long Parliament was not dissolved in 1641, why England divided into parties,
5 why there was no serious negotiation to avoid war, and why respect for majesty came to be so deeply diminished ... This conjunction was the result of three long-term causes of instability – the problem of multiple kingdoms, the problem of religious division, and the breakdown of a f:nancial and political system in the face of inflation and the rising cost
10 of war ... No one, or even two of these forces was enough; it took the conjunction of all three to drive England into civil war ...

It was never likely that any agreed settlement could be made after the end of the Civil War, because the negotiations involved too many different parties pursuing incompatible objects. Even with real political
15 skill on all sides a settlement would have been difficult to achieve ... [but] Charles I, Denzil Holles, the Scots' leaders, and John Lilburne all belonged to that school of thought which holds that the proposition that politics is the art of the possible is not merely open to abuse, but actually sinful. The only one of the participants in the search for a set-
20 tlement who was willing to take account of the limits of possibility was Oliver Cromwell ...

Comparative Chart of the Main Peace Terms

	Nineteen Propositions	Oxford Propositions	Uxbridge Propositions	Newcastle Propositions	Heads of the Proposals	Four Bills
Parliaments	Triennial Act stands	Triennial Act stands	Triennial Act stands	Triennial Act stands	Triennial Act repealed; biennial parliaments	Triennial Act stands
Privy Councillors	Parliament to approve	—	—	—	—	—
Officers of State	Parliament to approve 16	—	Parliament to nominate 13	Parliament to nominate 13	Parliament to nominate for 10 years	—
Militia	King to accept Militia Ordinance	King to settle with Parliament's advice	To be settled by Commissioners named by parliament	Parliament to control for 20 years	Parliament to control for 10 years	Parliament to control for 20 years
Church government	Reformed with Parliament's advice	Bishops, etc. Abolished	Bishops etc. Abolished reforms advised by Westminster Assembly	Bishops etc. Abolished; Presbyterian church for 3 yrs	Bishops etc. Cannot coerce; no Presbyterian church	Bishops etc. Abolished; Presbyterian church for 3 yrs
Papists	Existing laws to be enforced	Existing laws to be enforced	Existing laws to be enforced	Existing laws to be enforced	Existing laws to be abolished & new ones made	Existing laws to be enforced
Royalists not to be pardoned	—	2	58	58	7	58
Dismissals from office	—	2 for life	48 for life	48 for life	Parliament's enemies for 5 yrs	48 for life

Further Reading

The Introductory chapter covers a very wide period and you may want to find out more about these events. There are a number of very helpful books and resources. The Access to History series includes two outline studies of the period, in the *Contexts* series, published by Hodder and Stoughton. These are: A. Anderson and A. Imperato, *Introduction to Tudor England*, and A. Anderson, *Introduction to Stuart Britain*. Both of these contains lists of the various Access volumes related to the period, which offer more depth and detail. More advanced studies of the long time period are offered in A.G.R. Smith, *The Making of a Nation, 1500–1660*, and Conrad Russell, *The Crisis of Parliaments, 1509–1640*. There are also some good videos available, such as the relevant episodes of Simon Schama's *History of Britain*, and many useful websites. A huge range of traditional text books and studies offer more detailed investigations, and some are included or indicated in the bibliography at the end of the book, for those who want to study the period in depth.

An enormous amount has been written about the Civil Wars, much of it still controversial. It is therefore difficult to provide either a bibliography which is in any way exhaustive, or to provide a brief list which does justice to the different arguments and viewpoints. What is offered below is a list of suggestions that students might follow in order to study the period in greater depth, either as a whole or by picking out particular aspects for further investigation. The suggested works include a range of interpretations, so that the different schools of thought are represented. Hence they include some interpretations with which this author is not entirely in agreement – the aim being that students should read, consider and evaluate the different arguments for themselves.

Anyone who wishes to understand the history of the Civil Wars would find it useful to dip into some of the classic works on the subject, not because the interpretations have gone unchallenged, but because it is these interpretations and the desire to challenge them that have shaped the work of more recent historians. The first general account of the wars: Clarendon's *History of the Rebellion* (first published in 1702–4) is still widely available in good libraries, as is S.R. Gardiner's *History of England, 1603–56* (1893–6). A very readable biography of Cromwell was produced in 1900 by Gardiner's friend and defender, C.H. Firth, while his work on Cromwell's Army (1902) provides a useful starting point from which to consider more recent interpretations. Both books were later re-published in paperback. Finally, students who wish to understand why puritanism could be seen, by contemporaries and historians, as a challenging and revolutionary creed, could read the work of William Haller in his *Rise of Puritanism* (first published 1938, paperback edition by Harper Torchbooks, 1957) as well as his *Liberty and Reformation in the Puritan Revolution* (Columbia University Press, 1955).

More recent historiography can be usefully summarised within a number of categories.

General surveys – An introduction to the period is offered in Angela Anderson's *Stuart Britain* (Hodder, 1999) in the Access Contexts series. Barry Coward's *The Stuart Age* (Longman, 1980) is still useful, but has been complemented by his later volume, *Stuart England* (Longman, 1997) which adopts an issue-based structure. Roger Lockyer's *The Early Stuarts* (Longman, 1989) still has merit. Among older works, Christopher Hill's *Century of Revolution* (Nelson, 1961) remains useful. Its approach and interpretation has been challenged, but it remains a mine of information. A clear and accessible account of the period is given in Derek Hirst, *Authority and Conflict* (Edward Arnold, 2nd ed. 1987) while an accessible account that focuses on the war and Interregnum is provided in G.E. Aylmer's *Rebellion or Revolution* (OUP, 1987). A number of wider surveys which attempt to set the seventeenth-century crisis in a long-term context are offered by A.G.R. Smith, *The Emergence of a Nation State* (Longman, 1984); Conrad Russell, *The Crisis of Parliaments: English History, 1509–1660* (OUP, 1971); and R. Ashton, *Reformation and Revolution, 1558–1660* (OUP, 1984); Jonathan Clark's *Revolution and Rebellion: State and Society in England in the Seventeenth and Eighteenth Centuries* (Cambridge, 1986) has subjected earlier interpretations to severe criticism, but has itself been the subject of critical reviews. The student should judge for him/herself. An interesting fresh interpretation of the period is offered by J. Goldstone, *Revolution and Rebellion in the Early Modern World* (University of California, 1991), which looks at both the English and French revolutions in the light of demographic changes and their effects on society. While it is not suggested that this is essential reading, it does offer a possible synthesis of many recent conflicting arguments.

The causes and outbreak of the war have been the subject of many conflicting interpretations. A long-term, determinist approach is presented in Lawrence Stone's *Causes of the English Revolution* (Routledge, 1972) and challenged in the work of Cust and Hughes, Ashton and Fletcher. Of particular value are R. Ashton, *The English Civil War, 1603–1649* (1978); Ann Hughes, *The Causes of the English Civil War* (Macmillan, 1991) and Anthony Fletcher's massively researched *Outbreak of the Civil War* (Arnold, 1981). In addition, the serious student should read at least one of the publications by Conrad Russell. His revision of some earlier interpretations is characterised by its measured tone and balanced argument. Moreover his emphasis on the need to consider developments in Britain as a whole has introduced a new dimension and a genuinely original approach to the study of the period. His major work in recent years has been *The Fall of the British Monarchies, 1637–42* (Clarendon Press, 1991) but students may gain some awareness of his work from some of the collections of essays discussed below.

The approach to war and the political factions involved is addressed by J.H. Hexter, *The Reign of King Pym* (Harvard University Press, 1941). Again the interpretation has been challenged but the book remains of interest. There has been much debate about the emergence of different parliamentary groups, but there is no authoritative study of the presbyterian and independent groups. However, the issue is addressed by Derek Hirst, and in studies of the army by Austin Woolrych, *Soldiers and Statesmen* (Clarendon Press, 1987), and Mark Kishlansky. Kishlansky's argument in his *Rise of the New Model Army* (CUP, 1980) that religion played little part in motivating the New Model remains controversial. The most balanced analysis of this issue is offered by Ian Gentles in his *The New Model Army* (Blackwell, 1992). Those with an interest in military history will find J.P. Kenyon and Jane Ohlmeyer [eds.] *The Civil Wars* (OUP, 1998) an interesting collection of essays. Also useful on the war itself is Christopher Hibberts *Cavaliers and Roundheads* (HarperCollins, 1999), written in an accessible, even chatty vein. Parliamentary factions have also been studied in depth by David Underdown, *Pride's Purge* (OUP, 1971) and Blair Worden, *The Rump Parliament* (CUP, 1974). The best study of the royalist groups is Ronald Hutton, *The Royalist War Effort* (Longman, 1981). An alternative approach to the Civil War is offered by local studies. Most counties have been investigated, and the list is far too long to be included in full here. However, R.C. Richardson's *Debate on the Civil War Revisited* (Routledge, 1991) lists most of them, as well as being a useful introduction to the historiography of the period. An excellent survey is provided by John Morrill's *Revolt of the Provinces* (ed. 2nd Longman, 1998) which deals with the importance of local loyalties and neutralism in the Civil Wars.

Many attempts have been made to study radicalism and the role of the population as a whole. The attitudes of ordinary citizens were studied by Derek Hirst and Brian Manning in *English People and the English Revolution* (Heinemann, 1976) and David Underdown's *Revel, Riot and Rebellion* (OUP, 1985) developing the issues more fully. Radical groups are outlined in Frances Dow's *Radicalism in the English Revolution, 1640–1660* (Blackwell, 1985) and analysed in J.F. McGregor and B. Reay eds. *Radical Religion in the English Revolution* (OUP, 1984). Christopher Hill's monumental *World Turned Upside Down* (Penguin, 1975) is vastly informative. There are many excellent, and some over-enthusistic studies of the Levellers. One of the most accessible and balanced surveys is Howard Shaw, *The Levellers* (Longman Seminar Studies, 1973).

A final category of recommended reading is defined by the type of publication rather than content. There are a number of useful collections of primary sources. H. Tomlinson and D. Gregg, *Religion and Society in Revolutionary England, 1640–60* (Macmillan, 1989) includes a useful introductory commentary, while Ann Hughes, *Seventeenth Century England, Vol. I* (Open University, 1980) limits comments to specific information about the sources. John Morrill and David Smith have produced a useful volume of documents on Charles I (CUP, 1988) while the Longman Seminar Studies series includes volumes by Martyn Bennett [*The English Civil War*] and C. Quintrell [*Charles I*]. Many students also find biographies to be a useful way of studying the period. Pauline Gregg's *Freeborn John* (Dent, 1986) is the best biography of John Lilburne, and she has also written accessibly on Charles I, re-published in paperback by the Phoenix Press in 2000. Charles Carlton has produced biographies of Laud (Routledge, 1987) and Charles I (Routledge, 1983). The most charismatic figure, however, appears to be Oliver Cromwell. Of the many accounts of his life, Christopher Hill's *God's Englishman* (Weidenfield & Nicolson, 1970) remains highly readable, while Barry Coward's *Oliver Cromwell* (Longman, 1991) is clear and balanced. A recent publication by D. Smith, *Oliver Cromwell* (CUP, 1991) uses primary sources to construct a biographical account. There is also an excellent collection of essays edited by John Morrill entitled *Oliver Cromwell and the English Revolution* (Longman, 1990) which highlights particular aspects of Cromwell's life and career. The historiography of the period includes many collections of this kind. Conrad Russell's *Origins of the Civil War* (Macmillan, 1973) and John Morrill's *Reactions to the English Civil War* (Macmillan, 1982) contain contributions by many of the historians named here, and provide relatively easy access for students who already have a grasp of the main issues, and outlines of the major arguments and debates. Other essay collections such as Russell's *Causes of the Civil War* (Clarendon Press, 1990), Morrill's *Impact of the Civil War* (History Today, 1991) and *Nature of the English Revolution* (Longman, 1993) are equally useful. Although written by a single historian, their chapters address different issues and summarise debates in such a way that they can be used in separate sections. For students who have a heavy workload and find it difficult to work through books in a coherent way, these collections offer a user-friendly introduction to wider reading. A similar function is performed by articles and journals. There is clearly no space here to itemise separate articles, but the journal History Today has sought to encourage debate for many years, and a look through back numbers for the last decade would reap a rich and accessible harvest for those interested in extending their knowledge of the period.

Index